Birdwatching in Yorkshire

Birdwatching in Yorkshire

by R. F. Dickens
and W. R.Mitchell

DALESMAN BOOKS
1978

The Dalesman Publishing Company Ltd.,
Clapham (via Lancaster), North Yorkshire.

First published 1977
Reprinted 1978

ISBN: 0 85206 379 2

Printed in Great Britain by Galava Printing Company Ltd.,
Hallam Road, Nelson, Lancashire.

Contents

Illustrations

Cover picture of Puffins by R. F. Dickens.
Small drawings by Brian Waters. Drawing of Sparrowhawk on page 96 by David Binns. Photographs—Herman Hemingway, 49, 55, 56 (top); W. R. Mitchell, 50 (bottom); Arthur Gilpin, 51 (top), 54; G. N. Wright, 52; R. J. Stirrup, 53 (bottom); Ralph Chislett, 56 (bottom).

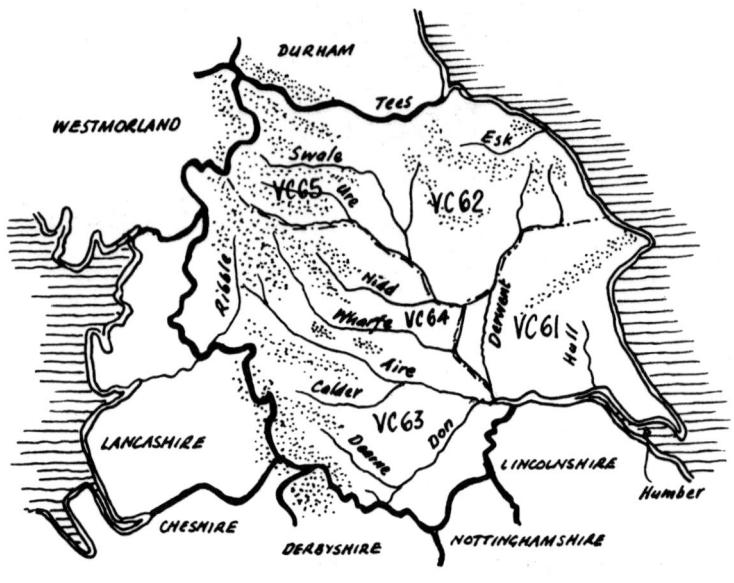

A general map of Yorkshire, showing the main river system, high ground and the Watsonian vice-counties.

Foreword

OUR aim in writing this book has not been to provide a standard work on the birds of a county. Between the definitive *Birds of Yorkshire* (Nelson, 1907) and its successor, *Yorkshire Birds* (Chislett, 1952), a period of 45 years elapsed. One of us had suggested, as long ago as 1968, that in view of the greatly increased number of observers and the volume of information accumulating from bird observatories, ringing stations and regularly-watched reserves, a 20 or 25 year interval would be more appropriate for the next major revision. Such a definitive work is currently in preparation and we look forward to its appearance.

In the meantime there are many people, both Yorkshire folk and visitors to the county who, while not the kind of serious students of birds to require the detailed information of a definitive work, are yet sufficiently interested in the countryside generally and in its bird life in particular to appreciate a book that will tell them what kind of birds they may expect to see in Yorkshire and in what types of habitat to look for them.

We have not attempted to provide a manual of bird identification. There is already an excellent choice of field-guides on the market, some indicated in our bibliography. Armed with such a book and this present volume, the reader should become reasonably familiar with the bird life of Yorkshire and, with some insight into the development of what has recently been claimed as the fastest-growing leisure activity, will not only enjoy his own birdwatching the more, but also will be able to make a contribution to the sum total of knowledge about birds in Yorkshire.

Our Study Area

DESPITE reorganisation in April 1974, Yorkshire has firmly retained its former identity, not least in the minds of Yorkshire folk. Although now classed as citizens of the County of North Humberside, the people of that area (the old East Riding) will claim that they are Yorkshire folk. Similarly, in the north, those who live in the Middlesbrough area still regard themselves as of Yorkshire, even though within recent years they have officially been, first in Tees-side and latterly in Cleveland. It is a matter of regret that the ancient term Riding has been obliterated, but the purpose of this book is not to argue the pros and cons of local government reorganisation. Suffice to say that birds pay scant regard to administrative boundaries imposed on local government, whether such boundaries are those decreed since April 1974, or for that matter those existing prior to reorganisation.

Watson devised a system of scientific recording in which Britain was divided into roughly equal "vice-counties". The Watsonian vice-counties 61-65 corresponded approximately to the former three Ridings and, ever since, have formed the basis for listing the county's flora and fauna and for detecting any changes in them. For there to be any meaningful comparisons, it is logical that the vice-counties, and consequently the pre-1974 Yorkshire, should continue to be used for such purposes. The Yorkshire Naturalists' Union has recognised the importance of continuing in this direction, and some years before local government reorganisation took effect it responded to the foresight of its then president, the late James Fisher, and declared its intention of retaining the Watsonian vice-county system.

For the purposes of this present work, we shall continue to regard Yorkshire in its old entity, bounded by the North Sea in the east; and, in the west, mainly by the boundary with Lancashire on the western slope of the Pennines. The Humber forms a natural boundary in the south, and the Tees a convenient dividing line between Yorkshire and County Durham, as our map indicates.

The size of the county is perhaps best conveyed by pointing

out that the West Riding *by itself* was larger than any other English county and that the North Riding, with something like 1,362,000 acres, came only close behind Lincolnshire and Devon, respectively second and third in size in the former county structure. The Pennines, often referred to as the backbone of England, in fact run north to south *within* the county rather than as a boundary between it and Lancashire. For the whole of its length from the Derbyshire border near Totley, the western boundary of Yorkshire follows Pennine moorland until it reaches its most northerly point at Cauldron Snout on the infant Tees. A diagonal, connecting Mickle Fell with Spurn Point, has a length of 120 miles.

As might be expected within a county of such size, there is a wide variety of geological and topographical features which in turn give rise to varied soils and vegetations, and consequently to the fauna dependent on them. A detailed account of geological and topographical matters can be found in the *Dalesman* book entitled *The Naturalists' Yorkshire* or in *The Geology of Yorkshire*, by P. F. Kendall and H. E. Wroot (1924).

Within Yorkshire, spurs of land extending west of the Pennines include the Howgill Fells in the Sedbergh area, and the Bowland Fells, the latter being most frequently visited by birdwatchers because Stocks Reservoir is an outstanding area for bird-life. The Pennines reach a height of 2,591 feet at Mickle Fell, in the extreme north-west of the county, and are cut by a series of attractive dales, including Teesdale, Swaledale, Wensleydale, Nidderdale, Wharfedale and Airedale.

The centre of Yorkshire is composed of a vast plain that is associated by name with the city of York; the plain extends northwards as the Vale of Mowbray. Dominating the north-east of the county are the Cleveland and Hambleton Hills, with small valleys such as Bilsdale, Bransdale, Rosedale and Farndale, all possessing a charm in every way equal to, but at the same time quite distinct from, that of the western dales. The moorland valleys run down to the Vale of Pickering, which separates them from the Wolds in the East Riding.

The scenic beauty of the moors and dales of the Pennines and the north-east is such that they were incorporated in two National Parks, named the Yorkshire Dales National Park and the North York Moors National Park respectively. The south-western part of the West Riding, west and north-west of Sheffield, lies within the Peak District National Park.

South of the Vale of Pickering and east of the Plain of York, the Wolds in effect cut off the low-lying south-eastern part of Yorkshire, which is known as Holderness, from the rest of the county. The Wolds are rounded chalk hills running from Flamborough Head to the Humber. They are dissected by a large number of valleys, most of which no longer contain running water. The boulder clay of the Holderness coast is being rapidly eroded by the sea, which carries the accrued, suspended material southwards to form the flat, narrow peninsula of Spurn Head at the mouth of the Humber. From the Humber northwards, the coast of the East Riding is low-lying until it reaches Flamborough Head, where the chalk cliffs mark the seaward termination of the Wolds. These cliffs—at Speeton, Bempton and Flamborough —have a maximum height of over 400 feet and are perhaps the most impressive mainland bird-cliffs in Britain. Further north, at Boulby, the Yorkshire coastal cliffs reach a height of 666 feet, the highest in England.

Yorkshire has over 3,500 miles of river. The Bain, which drains from Semerwater to join the Ure, is a mere 2½ miles long, but at the other end of the scale is the Swale, with a length of 83 miles from its source near the Westmorland border to the Vale of York, where it is joined by the Ure to become the Yorkshire Ouse. The Esk, which flows from the Cleveland Hills to Whitby, is the only river flowing directly into the North Sea anywhere between the Humber and the Tees. Even the Derwent, which rises within three miles of the east coast, meanders west and southwards for its 57 miles to join the Ouse between Selby and Goole, and thence continues—as do all other Yorkshire rivers—to the great Humber. The one exception (other than the Esk) is the Ribble, the upper reaches of which are in Yorkshire, but which continues westwards to the Irish Sea.

The county possesses few natural stretches of water of any size. Semerwater, lying above Wensleydale, is a notable stretch. Malham Tarn, near the head of the Aire, is better known and more frequently visited. Hornsea Mere, in the east, lies within half a mile of the North Sea. Water impounded by man to add attractiveness to country estates attracts many birds. Such lakes include Harewood, Bretton, Castle Howard and Sandbeck. On the western side of Yorkshire, where the rainfall is high, innumerable reservoirs have been created to serve the needs of Tees-side, the industrial West Riding and the south of the county. The reservoirs are attractive to many species of birds for feeding and roosting and compensate for the small number of natural lakes. Mineral extraction gives rise to flooded gravel pits and to what are generally known as "flashes", where mining subsidence has left areas of permanent floodwater. South Yorkshire is particularly rich in these features, and they in part make good the loss of swamps and marshes which once were widespread.

The lower reaches of most of the county's rivers flow for many miles through flat, low-lying ground. Castleford, at the confluence of the Aire and Calder, is still some 65 miles from Spurn Point yet has an elevation above sea level of only 50 feet. York, 45 river-miles from Hull (which is, in itself, an "inland" port some 24 miles from the mouth of the Humber), is below the 50 feet contour. These rivers, and adjacent low land, are frequently and temporarily flooded, especially in winter, adding to the watery spaces available to such species as duck and swan. So regular a feature was the flooded low country that the Viking raiders who sailed up the rivers and settled in this part of Yorkshire gave to the riverside washlands the specific name of "ings", which, as a close examination of the Ordnance Survey reveals, is a frequent suffix to place-names alongside rivers. Examples are legion. Fairburn Ings, Wath Ings and Wheldrake Ings will receive attention in a later chapter.

Yorkshire has two estuaries of any size—the Humber and the Tees. The area of the Tees estuary available for birds has been considerably reduced by reclamation and industrialisation but still remains an important ornithological site. Relatively speaking, the Humber estuary remains unspoilt but developments of one kind and another are periodically suggested. When there are storms in winter, Yorkshire harbours, especially those of Whitby and Scarborough, become noteworthy for their assembled birds.

Historically, Yorkshire was well-wooded. Trees extended well up the slopes of what are now bare moorlands. Remains of birch, oak and pine are found in peat deposits high on the hills. The clearance of woodland, and the effective deterrent to regeneration which the subsequent extension of sheep-rearing induced, have been off-set in recent years by extensive commercial planting. The Forestry Commission, in particular, has changed the appearance of vast tracts in North Yorkshire by afforestation, planting mainly the quick-maturing conifers. Wealthy landowners in the past had a less pressing need for a quick crop, and by planting deciduous species made their estates much more attractive to a variety of birds than is the case with the coniferous plantations. Old, decaying trees are necessary for the well-being of certain bird species, but today it is seldom that the full cycle is allowed to elapse to the stage where fungal and bacterial action restore to the soil the goodness which the trees originally abstracted from it.

The first impression of Yorkshire, derived by visitors who arrive from the south, is that the county is full of "dark, satanic mills", heavy industry and colliery spoil heaps. In fact, industry occupies a comparatively small part of the county, but it is appropriate for us also to consider these urban and industrial areas in relation to their bird-life.

Typical Nesting Species

Moor and Fell: The areas covered by this section are the wild, treeless "tops"—in the west, the Pennines, and in the north-east the North York Moors. Comparatively few species nest at high elevations, and a birdwatcher may have a tally of only three or four species during a winter walk. The springtime return of waders for nesting enlivens the high moors, mosses and upland pastures. Wader calls form the dawn chorus in areas where song birds are uncommon.

We judge from names like Plover Hill (adjacent to Penyghent) that the Dotterel, a wader only slightly larger than a Starling, nested on the Craven Pennines. This is no longer the case. "Trips" of Dotterel on migration to nesting areas much further north may be seen early in May on such peaks as Fountains Fell, Ingleborough and also high ridges near Wensleydale. The Dotterel does breed periodically on the Cumbrian Pennines. A distinguishing feature of the Dotterel is a prominent eye stripe, and a white band extends below the dark upper breast and above the chestnut and black of the upperparts. So confiding is the Dotterel that a human who takes care can approach it closely.

The Golden Plover—known as the "Pennine whistler"—nests at points all along the range. A small number of breeding pairs frequent the North York Moors. The Golden Plover favours stony, open areas, especially where mosses and lichen can provide camouflage for the eggs and young. A sitting bird's mantle of black and gold is inconspicuous in such a setting, though a few pairs nest on light green turf at the edge of Malham Moor. A wary bird, the Golden Plover slips from its nest well in advance of intrusion. Birds have been seen on the breeding grounds throughout the year, but the species is usually present on the hills from February until the end of summer. The Pennine birds are of the so-called southern race; it is less boldly marked on face and underparts than is the northern race, representatives of which, in flocks of up to 200 birds, may be seen in April, sometimes even in early May.

Smaller than the Golden Plover, but not unlike it at first glance, the Dunlin has been called the "plover's page". The Dunlin's preferred nesting area is a peaty plateau with some standing water at high elevation. On the Pennines it may be found on most ground above 1,500 feet. Like the Dotterel, the Dunlin is approachable by anyone who takes care. The displaying cock bird, flying high, utters an enchanting trill.

The excitable Redshank, once almost exclusively a bird of coastal marshes, has become well established on the Pennines, where it is characterised by a restless manner, flash of white on wings and rump and a yodelling call which becomes a resounding *chip, chip, chip* whenever anyone ventures near its young. Motorists using some of the hill roads become aware of the presence of Redshanks when they see birds perched on capstones of walls or the wooden uprights supporting strands of barbed wire. Snipe are frequently observed on such perches. Snipe sounds are among the most familiar in high, damp places. The "bleating" heard in spring as a bird makes a shallow dive high in the air is instrumental, caused by the air passing through the extra strong barbs of the outer tail feathers, which are extended for the purpose. At other times, an anxious Snipe may proclaim its presence with a *chipper, chipper* call. A bird flushed at close quarters takes to the air with what sounds like a short sneeze!

The Curlew, with its long neb and streaky-brown plumage, may be heard in most hill areas but during this century has nested increasingly on lower ground. The distribution of birds across the hills from traditional gathering places in the river valleys occurs in late February and March, and by August the adults and young of the year have returned to low ground, where the adults moult before migrating to the estuarial wintering grounds. One such assembly area is in the Ribble Valley, just below Settle. Malham Tarn often has a group of non-breeders in summer, and Gouthwaite in Nidderdale is notable for its wintering flock of Curlews. With its large size and long, decurved bill, the Curlew is easily recognised. The bubbling territorial call will quickly confirm the identification.

The Lapwing, known on the Pennines as "tewit", tends to frequent marginal ground characterised by ill-drained areas and beds of rushes, but—like the Curlew—a Lapwing may establish itself on better pastureland and meadowland at lower elevations. Dark in the body—a dark green, though in dull light it looks black—and with a jaunty head crest, the Lapwing stands out among the hill-nesting waders. The exuberant call of a cock bird at the nesting area is a typical sound at the moor edges in spring.

Typical of the heather moors the year through is the becking of Red Grouse which, alone of the hill birds, stay in their limited areas during the year, unless they are forced to leave by a cruel combination of snow followed by hard frost, which seals off their basic food, *Calluna*. At such times, packs of demoralised grouse may be seen in the dales. Yorkshire has some of Britain's finest grouse moors because there is heatherland at the right elevation, between 1,000 feet and 1,250 feet above sea level; and during the sporting era when the birds have been shot from butts a small army of gamekeepers has regularly burnt tracts of moor to provide fresh food and, in so doing, sustained the necessary monoculture.

The moors of Swaledale, Blea Moor and those around Wharfedale and Nidderdale (in the west), and northern parts of the hill land of the north-east, have been renowned for Red Grouse. On many hills, an example being Ingleborough, excessive grazing by sheep has removed the cover of heather. Any remaining grouse in such an area must subsist mainly on grass and the abundant rushes. The British Red Grouse, now generally accepted as a sub-species of the Willow Grouse, has been successfully bred in captivity but such birds lose their truly wild nature. The cocks become territorial and pair up in November.

In some areas, Black Grouse are regularly flushed with Red Grouse during the August drives. The Black is mainly associated with the hill edges, where the white (bent) ground is found, but in recent years has become locally numerous for a while during the early stages of afforestation with conifers. Black Grouse may be seen in open country around the head of the Tees (and also between there and Weardale), on and around Tan Hill, and in the far west, in areas lying near Malham and Settle.

Up to 30 birds have been reported from one Craven *lek*, where in the spring the cock birds gather for ritual display, accompanied by much cooing and hissing, and where in due course the females (greyhens) arrive. Further west, *leks* tend to be more numerous and of smaller size, with perhaps six cocks in attendance. The *lek* is most active and noisy at dawn, but late afternoon displays are to be seen at some of them until about the end of April.

The Short-eared Owl, an inhabitant of open country, is especially numerous in vole years, when there can be several pairs present in an area of new planting with conifers. This is a daytime-hunting owl which nests on the ground and commences incubation with the laying of the first egg, so that young in a brood are of unequal sizes; they are also very precocious and tend to move away from the nest before fully fledged. Short-eared Owls arrive on the moors as early as February and remain until as late as October. A conspicuous springtime display concerns the cock bird which, flying high, brings its long wings together beneath its body several times in rapid succession. Such behaviour may also be detected by anyone who wanders too near a nest.

The Merlin, a thrush-sized falcon, nests on moorland on the Pennines and in the north-east; a preference for gently sloping ground has been noticed. The Merlin is much less common than it was 40 or so years ago. Look for castings on moorland cairns. The Merlin's prey consists mainly of Skylarks and Meadow Pipits.

The Kestrel may be seen in hill areas where there are ruined buildings or old trees to provide nesting sites, but the raptors more closely associated with open moorland are the harriers—Montagu's (mainly in the east) and Hen Harrier (mainly in the west). Nesting takes place on a limited scale and harriers, from the north, winter in some suitable hill areas in Yorkshire, such an area being the upper Hodder Valley.

Of the crag-nesting species, the rarest is the Peregrine Falcon, which has suffered from falconers and egg-collectors and also (via its prey) has experienced a dangerous build-up of toxic substances in its body, leading to poor nesting prospects. The Buzzard nests in north-west Yorkshire, using cragface situations for the nest (some pairs further north have reverted to nesting in trees at the fell-edge). The status of this bird is directly related to the degree of persecution by gamekeepers and sportsmen; given freedom to nest it would soon move into the remoter parts of the Yorkshire Pennines. Few Ravens succeed in nesting, though there are periodic successes and broods are reared to independence. The northern Pennines is a good nursery area from which our Yorkshire stock could be replenished. Young Ravens from the northern Pennines appear in some of the Craven dales in winter.

A solitary tree on a moor or fell will possibly hold the nest of a pair of Carrion Crows, a common species. Nesting on thorn trees in small moorland gills is quite common, and near Settle, during 1975 and 1976, a pair of Carrion Crows attempted to nest on a walltop. (Crows' nests are occasionally used later by owls and even the Merlin). The Carrion Crow is the chief predator on the eggs and young of moor-nesting waders, notably the Lapwing and Curlew. This species is universally detested at the hill farms, which it visits in spring and, though possibly in the first instance attracted by the afterbirth of ewes in the lambing crofts, will not hesitate to attack ailing or weak lambs. One of the authors has the sad recollection of seeing a new-born lamb that still lived, though both its eyes had been plucked out by crows. Crows lag their twiggy nests with wool and, as in the case of the walltop nesting pair, use bones from a dead sheep as a nest foundation.

Moorland tarns attract Black-headed Gulls at nesting time. At some tarns, subject to sudden variation in water level, successful nesting occurs once in two or three years. Several thousand gulls occupy an island in Stocks Reservoir. The birds may fly a considerable distance for food, though a few have developed the knack of lifting trout from fell streams and, great opportunists, they attend any car parks or picnic areas in the locality. Black-headed Gulls "hawk" for larvae and insects over newly-cut hay at the hill farms. An estimated 200 acres of moorland not far from the Trough of Bowland holds a large gullery, but the species represented here are Herring and Lesser Black-backed Gulls, with a few Great Black-backed Gulls.

The commonest bird of the high hills—it is found in most localities—is the Meadow Pipit, which returns to the nesting area in mid-March, not long after the common Skylark. The nesting range of the Meadow Pipit extends from the felltops to the lower moors, and nests are not difficult to find, for the incubating bird frequently leaves just a little ahead of a human visitor, giving away the site. The Meadow Pipit is commonly the host to eggs laid by the parasitic Cuckoo. The Skylark is mainly a bird of the marginal land. Colonies of Twite—a species known in some Pennine locations as "mountain linnet"—may be found on the Southern Pennines. The Twite nests in areas of fairly rank heather or bracken. Out-of-season flocks may be seen on more northerly stretches of the Pennines.

Between late March and August, the Wheatear occupies many bare stony heights of the Pennines, and it is also a bird familiar to visitors to the north-east moors. The Wheatear, named after its prominent white patch at the rump, nests in outcrops of stone, sometimes in stone walls, and commonly in disused rabbit burrows.

The Ring Ouzel arrives from its North African winter quarters at about the same time as the Wheatear and also frequents stony country, such as scree slopes and steep-sided narrow gills on both the Pennines and the north-east moors. Commonly known as the "mountain blackbird", but readily distinguished from the Blackbird by reference to the white crescent on its breast, the Ring Ouzel's distribution is undoubtedly at higher elevations, though the reverse situation has been noted in a high area like upper Teesdale. Here, and in some other areas, Ring Ouzels have an inclination to nest in the disused mining shafts and levels. Before leaving the hills in autumn, small flocks of Ring Ouzels may be seen ranging the hill slopes to feed on the moorland berries, also taking the fruit of the Rowan.

Two species of duck may be found nesting at high elevation— at up to 1,500 feet on the Western Pennines. The Teal can be relatively common in some rushy areas of the Central Pennines but a visitor almost treads on the sitting bird before it betrays the nest. The Mallard's nesting range extends upwards to heather moorland. Both species prefer to nest not very far from streams.

Swifts from the towns and villages may be seen "hawking" insects over the hills during late spring and summer. Almost all the bird species leave the hills at the approach of winter, but then it is possible to see small groups of Snow Buntings, two favourite haunts being Ingleborough and high ground near upper Wharfedale, also on the Southern Pennines, where during the 1930s research into their visitations was conducted by John Armitage and others. They discovered Snow Buntings were visiting *mollinia* to feed on the clusters of gall-midge larvae infecting the haulms; Buntings also took the seeds of *mollinia*.

And in winter, even during snowtime, a bird-watcher in craggy areas may be surprised to be scolded by one of the smallest of British birds, the Wren.

The Dales: The word dale is derived from *dalr,* which is Norse for a valley. As far as we know, the exact number of dales in Yorkshire has not been established, but the figure must be well over 200. North of the Aire Gap, the dales allow moderating conditions to extend well into the hill country, and each dale has a number of minor valleys known as gills, running to even higher elevations. On the Southern Pennines, the smaller valleys are known as cloughs, whereas on the north-east Moors there is no specific name. A dale's tributary valley has "dale" in its title.

The north-western dales are generally large, bearing the U-shape of glaciation, bounded by high land. Although generally written of as being austere, they have a remarkable amount of indigenous woodland on their slopes; in the deep gills grow such native species as Birch, Rowan, Hazel. The Calder Valley is the only significant gash in the southern bloc, and this is deep and steep-sided, also well wooded. Dales in the north-east tend to lack the clean lines of those of the west; they are generally quite deep, with abundant ground vegetation extending to thickly-heathered moors.

No demarcation line exists between the hills and the dales across which the locally common birds do not stray. Hill-type birds may also be seen nesting in the dales; and the presence of the tributary valleys may encourage what are usually regarded as dale birds to nest at high elevation.

The Curlew, which last century was regarded as mainly a hill bird, is now more numerically strong in the dales, frequently nesting in the riverside meadows, its nest concealed by a rapid growth of grass. Changes in farming techniques, and especially the taking of grass as silage in two cuts, the first in late May, can cause a high mortality among Curlew young, and haytime tends to arrive when the chicks are only half-grown. (Such farming changes led to the decline to the point of extinction of Yorkshire-nesting Corncrakes). Curlews may be assembling in the lower

17

dales as early as February, and a movement to the wintering grounds occurs in late August, though traditional moulting grounds are known and, in these areas, cast Curlew gizzards may also be found.

The Lapwing, another familiar wader, has been referred to as a hill bird, though it is usually in marginal areas and, in the upper dales, may be found nesting down to riverside fields. So early do Lapwings return that they may be seen sitting hard during an April blizzard. Flocks of Lapwings can be seen as early as June (presumably they are of failed breeders). By September, immense flocks may be reported from low fields. where the Lapwings are frequently in the company of Starlings. Black-headed Gulls in attendance are quick to harry a Lapwing that has drawn food—a worm perhaps—from the ground. Low fields are later seen to hold flocks of Golden Plover which at first are still in nuptial black.

Within living memory, the Oystercatcher has extended its nesting range from the coast to take in the western dale country. It was a movement first observed in the early 1920s, when west coast Oystercatchers penetrated the Aire Gap, also the Lune, Ribble and Wenning. Oystercatchers nesting in Littondale are some 30 miles from the sea. The Oystercatcher is conspicuous in colouring and voice. This pied bird with the flesh-pink legs and orange bill can be inconspicuous when sitting on a nest made in a shingle bed beside a river, though in recent years a movement away from the rivers has been noted; nesting frequently takes place in fields. (Some early nesting pairs chose the six-foot between railway lines near Gargrave and Bentham). A six mile stretch of the Ribble surveyed in 1972 held over 10 pairs of Oystercatchers; only two pairs had chosen to nest on riverside shingle. Another riverside wader that can be numerically strong in the upper dales is the Sandpiper (which frequently finds safer and less disturbed nesting haunts by reservoir and upland tarn).

The Dipper of stream and river is as sedentary by nature as the moorland grouse; recoveries of ringed nestlings are rarely far from the point where they were hatched. The Dipper draws attention to itself by its metallic flight call, *zit, zit,* and an observer sees a stumpy, white-breasted bird moving fast at no great height. At other times, the bird perches, frequently with a "curtseying" movement, on a stream-washed stone, from which it ventures underwater to feed, using its wings for propulsion while in the stream. Its exploitation of food on the stream bed makes it possible for the Dipper to remain in the dales the year through.

A favourite site for the mossy, domed nest is a rock face; others are fond of nesting under stone bridges (but on girders under bridges at Settle and Gisburn Forest), and some nests

18

are so close to a waterfall they are continually splashed with water. The nuptial song of the Dipper can be heard as early as January, but the nesting season begins later on higher ground. The first egg is laid about March 27.

Dale country attracts many nesting wagtails. The Grey Wagtail nests by the reaches of streams—often, coincidentally, quite close to pairs of Dippers—and nesting can occur at an elevation of 600 feet. The first eggs may be found by mid-April and quite often this species is double-brooded. The upperparts of a Grey Wagtail are of slate rather than grey tone; the underparts are a brilliant sulphur-yellow. There may be some confusion with the Yellow Wagtail, a bird of the dales water meadows, which has greenish olive above. No confusion is possible between them and the well-named Pied Wagtail, which is generally distributed, choosing to nest in niches between stones, as on farm buildings or, frequently, drystone walls.

When visiting dales rivers, it is now worth looking for two saw-billed birds—the Goosander and Red-breasted Merganser. The former has nested by Tees, Ure and Wharfe; the latter in the upper Hodder Valley, also by the Ure. Kingfishers, which suffered a population collapse during the last severe winter, in 1962-3, and have been affected by the pollution of some streams, are again seen in many areas.

The farming revolution in remoter dales has resulted in the presence of many derelict buildings; quite often a number of small farms have been amalgamated and the area is ranched. Unused or little used buildings attract Stock Doves, Kestrels and Starlings. The Swallow and House Martin are equally at home in buildings still being used. Swallows frequently nest in cow-byres; House Martins build their mud nests under the eaves or against the tops of window frames. In the Craven district, where barns have generous porches, it is not unusual to find a colony of House Martins nesting against the rafters. (House Martins have been found nesting at about 1,000 feet above sea level using the stations of the Settle-Carlisle railway).

Green Woodpecker and Treecreeper, also a variety of tits, may be found in high-lying ash woods on the sides of dales, where natural regeneration of woodland takes place and rotten trees are not ruthlessly cleared away; there are thus good sites for nests and also abundant food. The Redstart is another distinctive nesting species in such open woodland conditions; this species may also be found nesting in drystone walls. At lower elevations, the mature stands of timber are good for warblers, and the Pied and Spotted Flycatchers may be seen. These species are present in Bolton Woods, by the mid-Wharfe, as is also the Nuthatch and the Great Spotted Woodpecker. The Hawfinch has bred occasionally.

19

Lowland Areas: The lowland section of the Craven district in north-west Yorkshire, noted for cattle-rearing and pastures, rather than arable land, consists of a patchwork of small fields which are enclosed by limestone walls in a part of the valleys of the Wenning and Ribble.

The former East Riding and the central area of Yorkshire comprise the vales of Mowbray, York and Pickering and consist in the main of rich agricultural land under more or less intensive cultivation but varied here and there by large country estates and pockets of woodland. Most of the latter are deciduous or mixed woodlands, more mature than the newer coniferous plantations of upland areas. A somewhat similar pattern obtains on the Wolds and it is convenient to consider them here as typical of a lowland habitat. The birds of woodlands will be dealt with in a subsequent chapter, as will the man-made lakes which, like woodland, are a feature of many of the large country estates. In these lowland areas east of the Pennines, hedgerows divide up the land: but in many areas hedges have been removed to create larger units for cultivation.

Rough grazing, particularly where low-lying and marshy, will produce bird species that we have already seen both on the moors and in the dales. Snipe nest earlier at this lower elevation. In the eastern areas they are, like Curlew and Redshank, less conspicuous than when breeding on the open moors but, in the Craven lowlands, limestone walls are often used for perching and it is possibly the best part of the county to see Curlews and Redshanks. As the end of the breeding season approaches, flocks of Curlews assemble as, for instance, near Austwick Moss. Another wader to be found nesting in Craven, but less frequently in the east, is the Oystercatcher.

Snipe are possibly more numerous east of the Pennines and their numbers are augmented at the end of the breeding season when their kind come down from higher ground and others arrive from overseas. Among other places, Fairburn, Birkin, the Derwent Valley and the general area of the new Selby coalfield may hold large numbers from early autumn and throughout the winter. It is not uncommon to find as many as 75-100 in one marshy field, a total not suspected until they are flushed and zig-zag away with a series of *scape* notes.

The monotonous song of the Reed Bunting is a feature of summer days, though as a species it is not confined to the lowlands. The cock bird, looking very smart with his jet black head, white moustache and collar, and chestnut back, perches conspicuously on favourite "song-posts". If disturbed from near the nest, the birds flutter off with outspread tail revealing white outer tail feathers.

Tussocky grass will provide sites for the well-concealed nests and turquoise eggs of Whinchats, more common in the east than in Craven. The birds themselves use wires, taller vegetation and low bushes for perches and song-posts. Where such bushes are sufficiently numerous to provide a kind of scrubland, Whitethroat and Lesser Whitethroat are other summer visitors likely to be found and, in damper areas, Sedge Warblers will almost certainly be present. The tussocky grass may also be used by Grasshopper Warblers. Their nest is even better concealed than that of the Whinchat and they do not reveal themselves by conspicuous perching. The ear, rather than the eye, will tell us if Grasshopper Warblers are present, but even when the curious reeling "songs" are heard it is difficult to locate the birds. Not only are they secretive but their song has a ventriloquial quality about it.

Skylarks frequent such rough areas in addition to the better cultivated land and richer pastures which Yellow Wagtails and Corn Buntings seem to prefer. The wheezy song of the latter is frequently uttered from roadside bushes and wires, in the same sort of areas where both the Common and Red-legged Partridges are most numerous—that is, in the south-eastern quarter of the county. The more colourful, larger, introduced Red-legged Partridge is often referred to as the French Partridge, or simply the "Frenchman". It is said that partridge are becoming less plentiful in some parts of the country. The true position is confused through the practice of rearing and releasing partridges, together with Pheasants, for the purpose of providing "sport".

Traditionally, lowland fields in the east have been enclosed by hedgerows; and the Wheatears and Pied Wagtails which inhabit the boundary walls in dale and moorland country and in lowland Craven districts are here replaced by Linnet, Greenfinch, Yellowhammer, Dunnock, etc. With the deplorable widespread eradication of hedgerows, such hedge-nesting species may find refuge in areas of scrubland; the importance to wildlife of uncultivated corners cannot be too strongly emphasised. Goldfinches and Bullfinches have both become commoner, the former especially where thistles have not been controlled or where burdock seeds are available.

The farmland is the larder for Rooks, which may nest in hedgerow trees as well as in woods and suburban areas. Not that the Rooks' feeding is necessarily frowned on by the farmer. Certainly the birds take grain but, against this, must be weighed their consumption of harmful wireworms and leather-jackets over a comparatively longer period of the year. The activities of Gulls, particularly of Common and Black-headed Gulls in winter when they follow the plough, underline the useful role which many species fulfil in ridding the land of unwelcome pests. Daytime roosts of these Gulls are often seen on farmland during the winter months.

Vast flocks of Lapwings and Golden Plover may frequent the same sort of areas, often several hundred strong. The quantities of invertebrate food needed to sustain them throughout the winter must be colossal, more especially when one recalls that winter flocks of Skylarks number hundreds. Fieldfares, Redwings and Starlings from northern Europe have also to eke out an existence, mainly in the same sort of areas, once the berries have been consumed. When ploughland and pastureland develop wet patches in a particularly rainy season, or after a thaw, Dunlin also join these throngs of birds in many parts of east Yorkshire.

In winter, the Reed Buntings, which we have already looked at, associate freely with Linnets, finches and sparrows, often in large flocks; they feed on weed seeds or spilt grain. The tail-corn attracts such birds as Mallard and, for a short period after their arrival from Icelandic breeding grounds, the flocks also of Pink-footed Geese, roosting in the Humber Wildfowl Refuge. These geese use Wolds arable rather than the more strictly lowland areas.

The winter flocks of small birds often have a preponderance of Tree Sparrows. The name sparrow results in them being less appreciated than they deserve. With chestnut cap, white cheek with a black "beauty-spot", and neat black bib, the Tree Sparrow is a most attractive species. Tree Sparrows require old trees with holes for nesting. A series of hedgerow trees in open country often houses a thriving colony. In another area which appears to have identical conditions, the birds may be virtually absent. Tree Sparrows readily take to alternative sites such as holes in walls, and it is a pity that we do not exploit this propensity more, and encourage them—as they do in Sweden—by the provision of nest boxes. The same hedgerow trees which Tree Sparrows find so much to their liking are perhaps the likeliest places to see the non-native Little Owl, which has now become established throughout the county.

Great Bustards and Stone Curlews used to breed on the Wolds. They have long since disappeared. The Corncrake, which within living memory was a regular feature of both agricultural lowland and the dales, is fast following their footsteps. Only a few Corncrakes and Quail are reported each year.

Drainage dykes in lowland areas, where wide and open, can be frequented by Herons and Kingfishers. Where they are overgrown, Sedge Warblers, Reed Buntings and Moorhens are common; and where pollarded willows grow, the scolding *chay-chay* of the Willow Tit is heard. It is not restricted to willow trees but requires soft or rotten wood which is easily excavated as a nest-hole. In more south-eastern parts, where phragmites or reed-grass grows plentifully, the Reed Warbler is not uncommon; it is here at the northern edge of its range, however.

A number of well-known heronries exist in lowland Yorkshire where in some areas the bird is still called Heronsewe. It is of interest to note that among the items at a banquet provided by Sir John Nevile of Chevet, near Wakefield, High Sheriff of Yorkshire, to celebrate his daughter's wedding in 1526, were "two dozen Heronsewes."

Swallows and House Martins are no less common in lowland villages than in the dales. The latter nest even in the centre ot towns, as at Selby. Swifts similarly are common, but the Sand Martin is perhaps less common in lowland areas than along dales rivers, except where semi-artificial sites such as sand quarries provide ideal conditions. In one sand quarry near Great Heck we have known Sand Martins and Tree Sparrows to occupy adjacent holes.

Parkland with old trees often has large numbers of Jackdaws. Stock Doves need similar nesting-holes, and Tawny Owls will use this kind of habitat in more open country as well as woodland. Barn Owls are less often seen than Tawny Owls since, unlike them, they do not roost out in the open daylight. But they can frequently be seen in a car's headlights at night, and unfortunately they are often road casualties. When one begins to make enquiries, a surprisingly large proportion of lowland farms have their Barn Owls (white owls, as they are frequently referred to).

Large flocks of Woodpigeons invade farmland in winter. Several thousand may be seen together. They flourish as we provide extra food through an increase in arable acreage, also extra roosting and nesting sites in plantations. Perhaps their best feeding areas are those in the east. Hard weather in winter makes Woodpigeons a serious pest when they descend on such crops as sprouts in market-gardening localities. The birds can persist despite organised shoots.

Perhaps the most notable change in lowland areas has been the arrival, as recently as 1959, of the first Collared Doves, and their spectacular increase in less than 20 years from being an unknown species in the county to an abundant one in the eastern lowland half and a colonist in almost every corner of Yorkshire.

Kestrels are common, though perhaps less so than in the hill country. Modern trends have included exploiting the marginal land alongside motorways where the small mammals on which they feed are perhaps more numerous through the disinclination of four-legged predators to hunt them there. Kestrels have also made use in many lowland areas of the electricity pylons which are strung out across the countryside from generating stations such as Thorpe Marsh, Eggborough, Ferrybridge and Drax. Carrion Crows may also use such nesting sites.

A number of commons such as Allerthorpe, Strensall and

Skipwith are to be found in the plain of York; and in the south and east is carr-land. It occurs especially between Doncaster and Goole and in the valley of the river Hull. Typical birds here include many of the species already discussed and others which are referred to in the section on Bird Haunts. Redpolls, which have increased in number in recent years, are fond of lowland commons and carr-lands where silver birches predominate, and where summering Tree Pipits and Warblers join resident Tits, Yellowhammers, Dunnocks and Wrens.

The lowland areas provide the best chances of seeing migrant waders in April-May and July-September but it will be more appropriate to consider these under water habitats. The passage of other, smaller birds is perhaps less easily detected; but examination of the flocks of small birds where crops have been harvested or where weeds abound among late potatoes, sugar-beet etc., will frequently reveal the presence of Wheatears, Whinchats and other species which we know are not local birds and which soon move on. Meadow Pipits are sometimes quite numerous.

Where boundary hedges have not been too severely cut back, a crop of berries attracts Fieldfares and Redwings, together with the resident Blackbirds, Song Thrushes and Mistle Thrushes. Stonechats come rather later than the Wheatears and Whinchats. Stonechats stake out a territory and remain for the winter months. A feature of these shorter days is the evening flight to communal roosts of large flocks of Starlings, the steadier stream of Rooks and Jackdaws, or the purposeful lines and echelons of Gulls heading for their customary reservoir.

Industrial and Urban Areas: The greatest concentration of industrial areas is in the southern half of the county, mainly against the eastern slope of the Pennines, but extending up into a number of valleys within the Pennine Range. The industry is comprised chiefly of coal-mining, chemicals, steel and textiles. Heavy industrialisation is also a feature of Tees-side, but here it does not extend over so wide an area as in the former West Riding. Naturally the greatest concentrations of humans live within or near these same areas. North of the Leeds/Bradford conurbation, and to the east of it, the towns and cities are generally smaller and set against a rural background, but the spread of industrialisation is likely to follow the development of the new coalfields around Selby, which is at present a pleasant market town with a charming and ancient abbey and is surrounded by rich food-producing agricultural land.

At first consideration, it might appear that the central cores of built-up areas are completely devoid of bird-life other than groups of feral Doves, and the ubiquitous House Sparrows and Starlings. But, in summer, Swifts may be seen hurtling and

24

screaming overhead, and the birds use town as well as village buildings in which to nest. House Martins build their mud-cups under the eaves even in the centre of some towns and many of our earliest records of Collared Doves came from built-up areas, including Goole, Leeds and Doncaster. At present many Collared Doves regularly visit a flour mill in the centre of Castleford where they pick up spilt grain. In at least one suburban area, nests are regularly built at the tops of telegraph poles.

Kestrels regularly breed on Leeds Town Hall, on mill buildings, and on the winding gear at a number of collieries. Kestrels are also associated with motorways, and it is alongside such sterile ribbons of concrete and tarmac that many people most frequently see a Kestrel hovering. Another feature of the industrial age, the electricity pylon, provides yet another nesting place.

To return to central built-up areas; in the evening, well-known roosts of Starlings are seen. The birds come in from their day's foraging in the country to occupy the outside ledges of those same buildings from which human throngs have moved out at the end of their day's work. Bradford and Huddersfield have suffered from this problem—for problem it is, with an accumulation of droppings on city buildings. Gulls wing their way to roost, in all probability to a nearby reservoir, and a steady stream of Rooks and Jackdaws may be making for a communal roost at some distant woodland.

As the noise of traffic quietens, after dark, one can hear the calls of other species flying directly over the centres of even large conurbations. Redwing and Blackbird, calling in autumn, give a good indication of the volume of migration. Common Sandpiper, Oystercatcher, Curlew and other species not associated with towns, reveal by their calls that they are passing overhead. At such times, wet streets and roofs may appear like stretches of water, accounting for the discovery at first light of birds like the Leach's Fork-tailed Petrel in Castleford, or the Shag which—according to the 1952 Y.N.U. report—"walked into a workshop near the river at Wakefield and died." Little Auk, Gannet and Manx Shearwater are among other sea birds which have been found, storm-driven, in inland built-up areas. Usually such birds are weak and exhausted and in most cases do not survive.

Even the most unpromising areas have their small oases, a feature of urban bird life which is increasing with redevelopment schemes. Grassed areas around blocks of flats and offices frequently attract Pied Wagtails which, like Starlings, may roost in city centres. School playing fields are widely used by Common and Black-headed Gulls in winter. A useful project for a school or natural history group would be to log the numbers daily at specified hours.

Shrubs and trees that have been planted to screen buildings or to line roads are not infrequently berry-bearing species. Waxwings in winter visit not only coastal towns like Scarborough and Bridlington, but have been seen even in Park Square, Leeds. They are more frequently reported from suburbs where there are gardens with berried shrubs than they are from rural areas, perhaps because they are more likely to be seen there.

Built-up areas, then, are not deserts of brick and concrete completely devoid of bird life. As a rule, as we move out from the central built-up core towards the outskirts, we come across increasing areas of open space. Suburban gardens in residential areas, and parks, may provide the equivalent of open woodland where such species as Blackbird, Song Thrush, Robin, Dunnock, Wren and the titmice may be as numerous as, or more so, than in an equal acreage of genuine woodland. Boundary privet and other hedges supply nesting places for some species, particularly Linnet and Greenfinch, while lawns and cultivated patches provide food.

Goldfinches and Bullfinches have become increasing visitors to suburban areas. The former nest in fruit and ornamental trees and the latter appear most regularly when trees and shrubs are in bud. The tits are great opportunists and will occupy sites with but the slightest resemblance to their usual tree-hole nesting place. The increased provision of nest-boxes and of food in winter has encouraged them to "go to town." Even Great Spotted Woodpeckers are regular visitors to some bird tables.

It is perhaps because many of what are really woodland birds now occur in suburban areas that a species like the Magpie is also common there. This handsome bird is not likely to be overlooked. While going about its business of acquiring food it is largely unheeded in the country, but when it takes the eggs or young from the nest which a Blackbird has built close to the house, and which we the occupants have kept under observation, it is immediately condemned. Yet, considering the matter objectively, we note that the overall population of Blackbirds does not decline. We still have one or two pairs in the garden again the next year and the next; and though we deplore it when Magpies play their predatory role, we do not seem to be too worried at the sight of these same Blackbirds consuming beneficial worms. Mistle Thrushes which nest in some suburban areas are particularly bold in defence of their young, diving down with rattling calls at the heads of human intruders and scolding Magpies mercilessly. Rooks have learned to live alongside man. There is a rookery well within the built-up area at Whitby.

It is, however, to the adjuncts of industry and urbanisation that we chiefly look for our birds in these areas. The larger parks, provided for human recreation, can and should be virtual bird sanctuaries. Unfortunately, in some areas the pressures of human interference result in few birds breeding as successfully as should be possible. Sewage disposal is a necessary service, and while there are now few of the old type of sewage farms that were formerly so attractive to a wide variety of birds, several figure regularly in ornithological reports. Among them are Stanley S.F., Knaresborough S.F., Esholt and Knostrop. Gulls, Snipe and waders frequent them, while Starlings, Wagtails and Pipits may be just as much at the modern sprinkler-type filter beds as on the old time sewage farm. Swifts, Swallows and Martins often congregate in the area.

Open disposal tips of household rubbish attract scavenging Rooks, Jackdaws and Crows (including Hooded Crows in winter). Such tips, more than anything else, explain the vast increase of inland gulls. The rubbish tip is as likely a place as any at which to spot one of those rarer species, the Glaucous and the Iceland Gull.

The need for houses and roads results in sand and gravel extraction. Coal must be mined for heating. Old, abandoned gravel-pits which become filled with water are, like mining subsidence flashes, focal points both for migrating and breeding species. The former include a variety of waders; the latter, birds like Coot, Grebes, Reed Buntings and species of duck. Even the tips of flue-ash from power stations and of colliery waste, which may look completely sterile to us, have their quota of birds. A majority of our Yorkshire Little Ringed Plovers nest on colliery spoil heaps, and it was on such a site that the only pair of Temminck's Stints bred. Wheatears are commonly seen in spring and autumn, with the later spring birds, in May, clearly of the Greenland race. The White Wagtails seen in spring will also be heading for northern breeding grounds. Colliery spoil will not appear much different from ploughed land to a Lapwing, and where some vegetation has colonised the tips, Skylark and Yellow Wagtail may also nest.

Analysis of county bird reports makes it clear that, far from being places to avoid, the industrial areas provide a wealth of birds. The fact that there is a larger human population (and hence more observers) does not entirely explain why, excluding places like Spurn, records from the old West Riding area invariably occupy a greater part of annual county reports.

Lakes and Reservoirs: Yorkshire has few large natural lakes but many small tarns occur in the Pennines, and a visitor sees innumerable reservoirs and other man-made waters. Ornamental lakes occur on private estates, and examples are Carlton Towers,

Nostell and Coniston Cold. Flooded sand- or gravel-pits, and areas of mining subsidence, offer open water habitats. There is a growing awareness of their value as refuges for wild-life and of the attractiveness of water as an amenity feature.

Additionally, areas of floodwater (which are, in effect, temporary "lakes") occur in many valleys, more particularly in the winter months. You will find them in the Vale of Pickering (Thornton Marishes); in the lower Derwent Valley (Wheldrake, Aughton and Bubwith Ings); in the Ribble Valley near Rathmell; and in the lower Dearne and Aire valleys, among others. The margins of such winter floods attract large numbers of Gulls, Snipe and Lapwing, which find rich feeding on the worms and grubs forced from the security of their underground fastnesses by a rising water level. One may find a smaller Snipe that rises from underfoot without any *scape* and with a direct flight rather than a zig-zag. In many cases the bird drops to the ground again not far away. These differences between it and the Common Snipe mark it out as a Jack Snipe, a winter visitor from north-east Europe and Asia.

Floods may attract family parties or even whole herds of Whooper Swans, which have arrived from Iceland. The larger numbers of Bewick's Swan, a species breeding in Siberia, tend to occur in the later months, January to March. Both species graze on vegetation below the surface, as well as on dry land. Where the water is deeper, they may often be seen "up-ending" after the manner of the more familiar Mallard. When these temporary "lakes" occur during periods of migration, or when levels of permanent water drop at that time and expose mud, the margins attract waders. Dunlin and Little Stint, Ruff, Greenshank and Sandpiper may then be seen, or perhaps a vagrant species from the other side of the Atlantic. Perhaps more surprisingly, Blackbirds, Fieldfares and Redwings can often be seen searching the areas around floodwater, doubtless finding it easy to probe in the wet, soft ground.

Resident Coots and Moorhens, with lobed-feet and long toes respectively, to enable them to scour the soft mud for food without sinking in, can swim with ease to nests that are out of reach of land-based animals.

Surface-feeding ducks like Mallard, Shoveler and Teal dabble at the edges of the water or feed in the cover of the reedbeds at permanent lakes; the marginal vegetation provides shelter for their young and a retreat to which they themselves can retire in late summer when they reach their period of moult and become temporarily flightless.

For wildfowl when alarmed, the water provides sanctuary provided it is sufficiently large in area to enable them to put a safe distance between themselves and the threat. Even here birds may not be entirely safe. Though out of reach of land-based enemies, many ducks and Coots have fallen victim to a rogue Great Black-backed Gull which frequented Fairburn for several autumns.

Obviously the sanctuary which floodwater provides is equally as temporary as the floods themselves and to find a real refuge, the genuine waterbirds (i.e., those with lobed or webbed feet) habitually make for areas of permanent water, more especially to roost. Morning and evening flighting between roosting and feeding areas can be impressive. Many ducks do a lot of their feeding at night-time and roost during the day. Conveniently, the birdwatcher can observe them at rest on the water. Diving ducks like Tufted Duck and Pochard not only seek refuge and a roosting place on the open water, but obtain their food from it. They can exploit greater depths than dabbling ducks can reach even when they up-end. But even the diving ducks must resort to firm land or reedy areas for nesting. The only truly aquatic stage is reached by the grebes; they not only feed and rest in the water but also build nests floating on it.

During the winter, many birdwatchers are engaged in regular duck counts. Figures are sent to the Wildfowl Trust and help to monitor fluctuations in the populations of different species from year to year. They also give an indication of the pressures of shooting which any given species can stand. Although wildfowl are legitimate game, only authorised persons may take them and then only during a specified period.

Any large lake or reservoir will meet the birds' need for refuge; but the deep, steep-sided reservoirs, such as one finds in hill country, or other reservoirs with artificial banks, lack certain features which are necessary to meet another of the birds' needs. Natural lakes and shallow reservoirs with gently sloping shores have an opportunity to develop marginal cover in the form of reed-mace, phragmites, glyceria, and provide not only food and nesting places for waterbirds and shelter for their young, but also nest sites for land birds like Reed Warblers, Sedge Warblers and Reed Buntings. The first two are summer visitors. Reed Warblers make a nest slung hammock-like between the stems of phragmites. In Yorkshire the species is at the northern limit of its range on the eastern side of the Pennines. Sedge Warblers and Reed Buntings are more widespread, being less confined to watery habitats.

In the shallower parts of lakes, emergent plants such as mare's-tail, bulrush, water plantain and celery-leaved buttercup often flourish. Again their seeds provide a valuable source of food for wildfowl. Floating on the surface or below it are amphibious bistort, water crowfoot, potamogetons and the like, which also provide vegetable matter, while the permanent water also has an opportunity to develop a community of animal life including small crustaceans like daphnia, water-skaters and other scavengers which, in turn, meet the needs of diving ducks or provide food for small fish on which grebes, sawbill ducks and divers may subsequently prey. Those waterbound larvae which escape the attentions of both water birds and fish, and which eventually emerge as flying insects (gnats, midges, mayfly, caddis-fly etc.), then run an added gauntlet as Swifts, Swallows and Martins congregate over the water when there is a good hatch. At such times, Black-headed Gulls can be watched dipping low over the water in the manner of marsh terns, to pick off insects from the surface. As well as forming colonies in many wetland habitats lower down, these Black-headed Gulls also nest at some of the moorland tarns.

Few, if any, of the higher reservoirs hold the overall attraction for birds that characterise the lower, shallower waters, but many have Common Sandpipers nesting round them. Meadow Pipits from surrounding moorland, and Pied Wagtails nesting in dales buildings and boundary walls, may visit the water's edge to pick up insects. Migrant waders occur but, generally, are fewer and less varied than at lower levels. Perhaps the higher reservoirs score best when it comes to records of Common Scoters, sea ducks which are not infrequently recorded when they make a temporary halt during the course of their coast to coast movements in summer. Shelduck moving overland from the west coast, en route to moulting grounds on Heligoland Bight, are seen in late summer.

Gulls roost on many of the reservoirs in winter. Favoured stretches of water include Blackmoorfoot, Ardsley, Eccup and Leighton. The gull roosts, unlike those of ducks, are confined to the night hours, and several species may be involved. Black-headed and Common Gulls are usually the most numerous. Ringing recoveries indicate that many of them have arrived here for the winter from Baltic countries. Black-headed Gulls ringed as nestlings in Latvia and Finland have been found in winter near Hull and Beverley. From Sweden, Denmark and the Netherlands they have reached Whiteholm Reservoir, Knaresborough and Fairburn respectively. The increased numbers of Herring, Lesser Black-backed and Great Black-backed Gulls which have been attracted inland by our refuse dumps are reflected in the higher numbers of these same species which now roost on our lakes and reservoirs. In general they are less common than the other two. The various species tend to split up into their own species groups on the water where rarer individuals, Glaucous and Iceland Gull, may occasionally join them.

Little Gulls, on the other hand, occur rather as migrants and are most frequently reported in early May after easterly winds, at a time when Black Terns may also be seen hawking over the water for insects. Other species of terns pass through. Sightings are mainly at lakes and reservoirs.

The man-made lakes on private estates are, in effect, bird sanctuaries. In the past these ornamental lakes demanded ornamental, introduced species, hence the origin of our non-native Canada Geese. The large Yorkshire population of these birds is still mainly based on such areas. Swinton Park, Castle Howard, Bretton, and others, have their flocks which sometimes increase to embarrassingly large numbers and necessitate periodic culling.

Nesting Great Crested Grebes are happily now more numerous than they were last century when persecution for "grebe-fur" reduced the population for the whole of Britain to just over 30 pairs in 1860—a number now exceeded annually in Yorkshire alone. In winter a few grebes remain inland until hard frosts force them to join the majority which have already made for coastal waters. While open water remains, the breeding ducks like Mallard, Teal, Tufted and Pochard will be joined by others of their own species from further north and east.

With these will come other species which, apart from odd individuals, have been entirely absent since the previous April. Goldeneye and Goosander occur regularly on many lakes and reservoirs in winter; the Smew, Long-tailed Duck and Scaup are seen less frequently and in smaller numbers. Diver, Shag and Cormorant may also be seen occasionally, the last-named occurring regularly at Hornsea, near the coast. Rarer grebes like the Slavonian and Red-necked Grebe may join the Great Crested and Little Grebes which have nested here.

In many ways our lakes and reservoirs become more exciting and hold more interest for the birdwatcher in the winter months, when not only are additional species of water birds present but there is also the challenge of changing plumages to identify.

Deciduous and Coniferous Woodland: The increase in the amount of deciduous and mixed woodland as one comes further down the dales is accounted for in part by large estates on which woods and copses were planted in past centuries. Mature timber is necessary to species such as Treecreeper, Woodpecker and Nuthatch. The latter is not uncommon in some areas but is a strangely local species and entirely absent from some mature woodland which appears quite suitable. Where it occurs it is often noteworthy for its tameness. In some places, Nuthatches come readily with tits and Chaffinches to feed near parked cars. In addition, Hawfinch, Jay, Tree-creeper, Long-tailed Tit and, in summer, Tree Pipit and Spotted Flycatcher inhabit these woods. The Pied Flycatcher is perhaps more commonly found in the dales in wooded areas, near to rivers and streams.

Suburban gardens and parks may be regarded as equivalents to open woodland. Birds like Blackbird, Song Thrush, Robin, Wren, Hedge Sparrow or Dunnock, and the Tits which we observe daily from our windows are also found in woods.

The Great Spotted is probably the commonest of the woodpeckers, since Green Woodpeckers suffered a marked decrease following the severe winter of 1962-63 from which they have still not fully recovered. The Great Spotted is also the least shy and in some places visits bird tables regularly. Spending its time more in the tops of trees, among smaller branches, the Lesser Spotted Woodpecker is less often seen than the other two, but is probably more widespread than records suggest. Its call in spring is often the surest guide to its presence.

Some townspeople find it surprising that many Starlings nest, woodpecker-like, in holes in trees. Nevertheless a hole in a tree is the *natural* nesting place and it is because of the bird's extreme adaptability in using sites in man-made structures that Starlings have become so successful.

Woodcock, Tree Pipit, Willow Warbler, Robin and Wood Warbler nest on the ground within woods. Wood Warblers seem to have a preference for beech woods and sloping ground but they are nowhere as common as the other leaf warblers, the Willow Warbler and Chiffchaff, which like Garden Warbler and Blackcap are common in any woodland with a degree of shrub layer.

A good crop of beech-mast attracts flocks of Bramblings in winter. Bramblings are visitors from Scandinavia, as will be many of the Chaffinches which associate with them. In addition to being a winter visitor, the Chaffinch is also a resident species, still numerous in woodland areas in the dales although it has become far less common in lowland areas.

The most regular owl of deciduous woods is the Tawny Owl but it is also found in coniferous woodland, and in hedgerow timber of farmland.

A conifer blanket extends across many tracts of hill land in Yorkshire. Marginal agricultural land has become dense forest well within living memory. Stands of larch were being planted by private estates from about the 18th century—one of the first plantations of Japanese larch appeared on the Ingleborough Estate, based on Clapham, in 1914—but the truly large forests have appeared under the auspices of the Forestry Commission, which was established at the end of the 1914-18 war. The Commission began to plant "exotics", a number of conifer species brought from the north-west of America. In Yorkshire forests today, the sitka spruce predominates in the west and is found on wetter ground in the north-east, though Scots pine has become an important species of the lower hills.

An early venture of the Forestry Commission in Yorkshire was Gisburn Forest, in the upper Hodder (3,000 acres). By far the largest scheme involves the North York Moors, where the Pickering Forest District (some 30,000 acres) is now the largest forest tract of upland heath in England. It was established as recently as the 1950s. Other notable forests, planted by private commercial interests, include Greenfields (2,300 acres), on the gathering grounds of the Wharfe and Ribble. This forest forms a crescent just north of Penyghent.

A conifer forest is a relatively short-term enterprise; the trees quickly mature and are felled, when the cycle begins again. In transforming bare hills into forest, man accounts for some loss of bird species but as the forest develops the number and variety of birds increase. Bird-life is at its most varied in the early stages, when the conifers are yet a stubble on the hillside. Voles proliferate, attracting owls and hawks. In "vole years" several pairs of Short-eared Owls may nest within a short distance of each other. The Kestrel can be quite common where old buildings have been left standing or there are a few old trees. This successful hawk may also nest on quarry and rock faces. Harriers find suitable nesting grounds in young coniferous forests, and the Montagu's Harrier has used this kind of habitat in the northeast. Smaller birds seen in the early stages of a new forest include Whinchat, Willow Warbler, Yellowhammer and Meadow Pipit; and, where original tall trees provide song posts, Tree Pipits may occur.

In some western areas, the Black Grouse is relatively common, though birds may have to shift their *leks* with the coming of drainage channels between which trees will be planted. In due course, the Black Grouse will move to the peripheral areas. A young conifer forest can have a high population of Pheasants which move in from outlying estates. Barn Owls nesting in old buildings in a western forest spend part of their time hunting in open country (their normal custom) and the remaining time within the forest (where they fly up and down the rides seeking voles). Woodcock may be heard on their roding flights down the rides and at the forest edges.

As the forest matures, it becomes attractive to finches, especially Chaffinch and Bullfinch. Blackbird, Lesser Redpoll and Long-tailed Tit establish themselves. The Goldcrest can become numerous. A mature forest holds relatively few bird species. Sparrowhawks have a preference for larch plantations (having ready access to the nesting sites between the well-spaced trunks). Mature coniferous woodland is probably the chief stronghold of the Long-eared Owl. The Tawny Owl can be as numerous as food supplies allow. Woodpigeons become numerous to the point of being a pest; the peak populations are recorded in the west during good seed years on farmlands round about.

Because the conifer trees are generally young and vigorous, few opportunities exist for species with a preference for nesting in holes. Enlightened foresters, with some help from volunteer ornithologists, have initiated nest-box schemes, and it has been found that the Coal Tit is the species most commonly using such boxes. Great and Blue Tits readily take advantage of boxes, and in Gisburn Forest there is a record of one being used by a pair of Tree-creepers.

Facilities granted to the public to visit the forests of the Commission are prominently indicated on the approach roads. Visitors are expected to explore the forests on foot, but deep penetration by car is possible at two "forest drives"—Hackness to Thornton Dale and in Newton Dale, both in the north-east.

Estuaries and the Coast: Most of the Yorkshire coast consists of cliffs, ranging in height from over 600 feet at Boulby to relatively low and fast eroding cliffs in Holderness. Interesting waders and gulls periodically call at some of the deeper indentations on the coastline such as Robin Hood's Bay and the bays of Scarborough, Filey and Bridlington. Weed-strewn rocks attract wintering Turnstones and Purple Sandpipers. More sheltered waters afford views of grebes and divers. Some Eider and Long-tailed Ducks get this far south. In the areas of cliff, few tracts of tide-washed mud exist to attract the migrant and over-wintering waders. To be sure of seeing large flocks of these birds you must go to the great estuaries of Tees and Humber.

Teesmouth, which now has a massive industrial complex, retains some mudflats and sandbars on and around which birds can rest and feed. The Humber estuary is so vast it is often a matter of chance whether birds in sizeable flocks will be seen at close quarters. A high tide will encourage them to congregate at favoured sites. Each tide makes available a fresh supply of food, and the largest numbers of feeding birds exploit this source by following the receding tide as it exposes new areas of mud. A train journey along the north side of the estuary can be rewarding to anyone who scans the shore. The Shelduck is both common and conspicuous. Spurn Point, at Humber mouth, and the Humber Wildfowl Refuge, where the estuary is relatively narrow, are places to visit.

Pink-footed Geese visit the Wildfowl Refuge. Brent and other geese in small numbers are also reported from the estuary. Duck regularly seen at sea from Spurn include the Common Scoter, while the Humber foreshore sustains a wintering flock of surface-feeding ducks, mainly Mallard and Wigeon. Diving Scaup are sometimes attracted in numbers to points where crustaceans and molluscs are plentiful. The waders can be varied as well as numerous, with regular sightings possible of Oystercatcher, Curlew, Ringed Plover, Bar-tailed Godwit, Turnstone, Sanderling and Grey Plover, but with Dunlin, Knot and Redshank as the most numerous species. At migration time, the following may also be present: Whimbrel, Curlew Sandpiper, Little Stint, Ruff, Greenshank, Spotted Redshank. Birds of the winter shore include Snow Bunting and Shore Lark and flocks of Linnets, buntings and finches, among which Twite may sometimes be found.

The cliffs at the northern part of the Yorkshire coast are impressive but not outstanding for their bird life. Herring Gulls are thinly-spread; they also nest on rooftops at Whitby and Scarborough. In 1976, counts revealed 348 and 143 nesting pairs respectively. The first large seabird colony to be seen by anyone who journeys south is at Castle Cliff, Scarborough, the nesting place of well over 1,000 pairs of Kittiwakes. Birds launch themselves into an uprushing wind to sail serenely over parked cars and promenaders to gain the open sea. The Fulmar is a conspicuous nesting species on these Scarborough cliffs and Ross's and Mediterranean Gulls are rarities which have been seen nearby.

Filey Brigg is attractive to birds and a notable vantage point. A line of rocks extends from a headland like a breakwater. In winter, the Purple Sandpiper is present, also Eider and Redbreasted Merganser. Snow Bunting and Shore Lark are attracted by the seeds of spurrey growing on the cliff top, and finches, especially flocks of Greenfinches, dine on the seeds of sea rocket.

Look southwards from Filey and you see the termination of a great ridge of chalk extending across south-east Yorkshire. These chalk cliffs rise gradually from Speeton to attain about 400 feet at Bempton, and though less high they are still impressive at Flamborough Head. The chalk tails off towards Bridlington.

Tenanting the chalk cliffs from about March to August is the largest congregation of seabirds on the English coast. At Bempton can be found the only English breeding colony of Gannets. Kittiwake, Herring Gull, Puffin, Guillemot, Razorbill, Fulmar, Shag—well over 50,000 birds in all—make full use of crannies and ledges to incubate eggs and rear their young. Then all but the Herring Gull disperse far out to sea. Great care is needed on the part of anyone visiting the cliffs, the short dry grass on the upper slopes offering no foothold. The cliff edge is unstable. Bempton Cliffs are in the care of the R.S.P.B., and during the nesting season a warden is present at an information centre.

The Kittiwake is the commonest species of seabird on this Yorkshire chalk; birds dally over the task of nest-building and it is ofen the middle of May before the eggs are laid. In Yorkshire, three eggs to a clutch is normal; the clutch size at colonies further north tends to be smaller. When the young have been reared, the Kittiwakes disperse far out to sea.

Fulmars glide on stiff wings at the rim of the cliffs to which the first settlers came as recently as the 1920s during the rapid spread of the species to all suitable coastal districts of Britain. Nesting pairs are now well, if thinly spread on ledges. Though superficially like a gull in appearance, the Fulmar is a petrel, with tube-nose, and it feeds largely on plankton which it gathers as it glides low over the waves.

Fenced off promontories at Bempton are handy look-outs from which to see the three species of auk: Guillemot, Razorbill, Puffin. Their colonies are quickly located by reference to the direction taken by incoming birds and also by the presence of rafts of birds off-shore. Guillemots crowd their favoured ledges, and birds that are incubating eggs or brooding young tend to be hunched in appearance and facing away from the sea. In summer it is possible to see the black-downed chicks; later, at dusk, adult birds below call to their young, which respond by launching from the cliffs and descending to join them on the sea, well before the time when they have learned to fly. The Razorbills, which are fewer in number, are seen where there are crannies in the rock, for nesting does not usually take place in the open. Puffins, which in other parts of Britain are mainly nesters in burrows on islands or cliffheads, are usually seen at Bempton and Flamborough where there are crevices in the rocks.

The Bempton gannetry lies to the north of the information centre and can be viewed by following a footpath to a promontory from which the nesting ledges can be seen. Gannets, probably of Bass Rock origin, were first seen at Bempton in the spring of 1924; this pair frequented the Black Shelf. A nest was seen in the following spring, and it is possible that eggs were laid then and in succeeding years but were taken by the cliff-climbers who, before a change was made in the law, collected thousands of seabird eggs as food and for the benefit of collectors. Positive proof of the Gannet nesting at Bempton was first secured in 1937. Two years later it was reported that four pairs were present. After a slow start, the gannetry became well established and now the estimated number of breeding pairs is about 130. The birds sometimes use nylon fishing-net in the construction of their large nests with disastrous results for some young birds which become entangled in it.

From these cliffs, from Spurn, South Gare and other vantage points on the coast large movements of seabirds can be watched, including shearwaters and skuas in late summer and Little Auks in winter gales.

Some Yorkshire Haunts

IN presenting this list, we would emphasise that seeing an expected species, however rare, in a *known* haunt has nothing of the thrill of exploring seldom-visited country and there discovering for one's self some unexpected bird. Our list is a selection only, and an arbitrary one. For example, we have been able to include only a *few* representative reservoirs.

We stress that its publication in no way implies a public right to access. Permission, if courteously sought in advance from the appropriate authority by a bone fide naturalist, is in most cases readily given. Any conditions imposed should be strictly observed for the sake of others who may wish to follow. The welfare of the birds must always be a foremost consideration.

Details of worthwhile areas, in addition to those mentioned in our list, can be gleaned from the annual ornithological reports published by the Yorkshire Naturalists' Union. A single grid reference should suffice to fix site locations.

SE 271414 **Adel Dam:** Near Leeds. Reserve extends over 20 acres, some mixed woodland and artificial lake, made by the damming of the Adel/Meanwood Beck. Leased to the Yorkshire Naturalists' Trust, with access restricted to members. Waterside species include: Canada Goose, Mallard, Little Grebe, Moorhen, with visits from Heron and Kingfisher. Woodland species: warblers, tits, Tawny Owl and Kestrel.

SE 761473 **Allerthorpe Common:** To the east of Allerthorpe village west of Market Weighton, including a reserve of 15 acres leased by the Yorkshire Naturalists' Trust from the Forestry Commission. Some heathland species: Nightjar, Curlew, Whinchat. In winter, the bird visitors include Snipe and Woodcock.

SE 043764 **Angram and Scar House Reservoirs:** Upper Nidderdale. Owned by the Yorkshire Water Authority who, since 1975, have allowed public access under certain conditions and during the main tourist season. Visitors are allowed to follow a four mile private road to a parking space within sight of Scar House dam, from which a footway leads to the dam at Angram, with a return on the other side of the water. Birdwatching permits to individuals are issued on application. Breeding and moulting waters for Canada Goose, Mallard and Teal. The geese are rounded up during the flightless period in summer for ringing. Three sightings of Golden Eagle reported. The surrounding area holds breeding stocks of Golden Plover, Lapwing, Red Grouse and Wheatear. Sandpipers breed by the water. The presence of migrating waders is in part determined by the amount of mud exposed.

SE 290250 **Ardsley Reservoir:** Near Wakefield. Owned by the Yorkshire Water Authority. Permits issued annually to the Huddersfield Birdwatchers' Club, R.S.P.B., Wakefield Naturalists' Club and individuals. Roost for gulls, mainly Black-headed, which are discouraged by the use of "scarers".

SE 011888 **Aysgarth Falls:** Upper Wensleydale. Inquire initially at the information centre of the Yorkshire Dales National Park, which stands not far from the north bank of the river. At Aysgarth, the Ure tumbles over three sets of falls, and stretches of the banks are richly wooded. The riverside birds include Dipper, Grey Wagtail, Common Sandpiper and Moorhen. The Kingfisher is becoming more common in Wensleydale and may also be encountered. Blackbird, Robin, Chaffinch and various species of tit, accustomed to the regular arrival of vehicles and the associated food scraps thrown out by the occupants, frequent the car parks. Nuthatches occur in nearby woodland. On adjoining stretches of the river occur Oystercatcher, Redshank, Mallard and Heron.

TA 197742 **Bempton Cliffs:** On the Yorkshire coast, north of Flamborough Head. A reserve of the R.S.P.B. Cliff Lane leads from Bempton village to a car park and information centre. Short walk to the cliff tops and the five miles of cliffs forming the reserve. A public footpath runs along the cliff top. Keep to the path or to the fenced-off promontories. *The cliffs are potentially dangerous to anyone scrambling at the edge and several fatal falls have been recorded in recent years.* The best period for a visit to Bempton is May to mid-July. At Bempton can be found the greatest concentration of seabirds on the English mainland. The main attraction today is the only mainland Gannet colony in Britain, with about 130 pairs. The colony is steadily increasing in size. Colonies also of Guillemots, Razorbills, Puffins and Kittiwakes. Shags nest at low levels where the tide has eroded ledges and caves. Doves are present in numbers. Most appear to have some "feral blood", but many approximate as closely to genuine Rock Doves as any on the English mainland coast.

SE 531266 **Birkin:** Near Ferrybridge, $3\frac{1}{2}$ miles east of the A1. Low-lying areas of mainly arable land on the north side of the Aire. Frequent flooding in winter months attracts Whooper and Bewick's Swans fairly regularly. Ducks commute between these feeding areas and the sanctuary at Fairburn for roosting. Impressive winter flocks of gulls, Lapwings and Golden Plover. Under suitable conditions, the area is good for migrant waders in late April/May and July/September.

SE 566331 **Bishop's Wood** (Selby Forest): A Forestry Commission "open" forest, with nature trail leaflet available. Tit species plentiful especially Coal Tit. Tree Pipit and Warblers in summer. Jay and roding Woodcock can be seen. In winter, Siskins and Bramblings roost in the area.

SE 095125 **Blackmoorfoot Reservoir:** A high reservoir in the Pennines, a few miles south-west of Huddersfield. A road running alongside makes for ease of observation. The owners, Yorkshire Water Authority, issue annual permits to the Huddersfield Birdwatchers' Club, R.S.P.B. and individuals. Ducks and waders frequent Blackmoorfoot Reservoir in season. Gull roost.

SE 845235 **Blacktoft Sands:** At the confluence of the Trent and the Humber. Reserve of the R.S.P.B. A vast reed-bed area, Blacktoft has Shelduck, Bearded Tit and Short-eared Owl among its nesting species. The Marsh Harrier is seen regularly from spring to autumn; it bred here in the early 1960s. Hen Harriers in winter. Blacktoft lies on the Humber migration route.

SE 088554 **Bolton Woods:** Upper Wharfedale. Mature woodland, mainly deciduous, along banks of the Wharfe. The Strid Nature Trail, west of the river, can be followed on payment of a small charge. Typical birds of the river include: Dipper, Grey Wagtail, Common Sandpiper and Kingfisher. Notable among the woodland species are: Nuthatch, Great Spotted Woodpecker, Green Woodpecker, Redstart, Pied and Spotted Flycatchers, Treecreeper, Wood and Garden Warblers.

SE 281124 **Bretton Lakes:** Near Wakefield. A reserve managed by the Yorkshire Naturalists' Trust. Nature trails have been set out, but advance permission for a visit is needed. In the woods may be seen Nuthatch and, with luck, the Lesser Spotted Woodpecker. Great Crested and Little Grebe are among the waterside nesting species.

SE 507168 **Brockadale:** In the Went Valley near Pontefract. A reserve of the Yorkshire Naturalists' Trust. Mainly botanical in interest, but nevertheless having a good list of woodland bird species, including Wood Warbler and Hawfinch. An interesting habitat, and additional species in the adjacent lower reach of the Went where, despite pollution, the Kingfisher is seen regularly.

SE 707365 Bubwith Ings: North of the A163, east-north-east of Selby. These ings are frequently flooded in winter by the lower Derwent; the floods and their birds can be viewed from the road, from the river bank or from near Aughton church. Under suitable conditions, the area carries large numbers of duck — especially Wigeon—and Bewick's Swans.

TA 053903 Castle Hill, Scarborough: About 1,000 pairs of Kittiwakes, also Fulmar and Herring Gull—all easily observed from the nearby Marine Drive. The cliff is crumbling; it is unwise to investigate the nesting colonies from the top.

SE 713707 Castle Howard Lake: Off the A64, 15 miles from York. Ornamental lakes in the grounds of one of England's most majestic country houses attract ducks, including Goosander and Shoveler; also Canada Goose. Osprey and Marsh Harrier are occasionally seen on passage.

SE 055516 Chelker Reservoir: By the main road between Skipton and Addingham. Strategically sited on a migration route, Chelker attracts a variety of duck, waders and terns; they use the water as a resting and feeding station, particularly when the reservoir's low levels coincide with spring and autumn bird movements. Tufted Duck and Coot are common outside the nesting season, and Goosander may be seen. Lapwings in large numbers gather round about. The Great Crested Grebe has nested.

TA 212216 Cherry Cobb Sands: On the Humber shore, south-east of Hull. A high-tide roosting area for waders, the sands are at their best in migration seasons. Besides the more common waders, such species as Curlew Sandpiper, Black-tailed Godwit and Ruff are seen.

SD 745695 Clapham Woods: Extending from the head of Clapham village, which lies just off the A65 between Settle and Ingleton. Small charge made for admission to the woods which, incidentally, contain groves of rhododendrons and bamboos planted by Reginald Farrer. The path from the village leads beside Ingleborough Lake and wooded gorge, thence to dry limestone valley, the setting for Ingleborough Cave. The lake holds a good stock of Mallard, which are reared for sport. Woodland species of birds include Woodcock and, latterly, the Jay. On the stream higher up are Dipper, Grey Wagtail, with Wheatear on and around the limestone outcrops.

SD 896556 **Coniston Cold:** Close by the A65 to the north of Gargrave. Private estate. Ducks visiting the lake include Tufted and Pochard and, especially in winter, Goldeneye and Goosander. Woodland species present include Treecreeper, Nuthatch and tits. Herons usually present.

SE 498009 **Denaby Ings:** A washland/marshland area in the Dearne Valley. Reserve of 35 acres administered by the Yorkshire Naturalists' Trust. Breeding species include Mute Swan, Pochard, Great Crested Grebe, Shoveler, Mallard, Little Grebe, Little Ringed Plover, Common Sandpiper, Tufted Duck, Yellow Wagtail, also many Reed and Sedge Warblers. Winter visits from Whooper and, sometimes, Bewick's Swans.

SE 300417 **Eccup Reservoir:** Near Leeds. The Yorkshire Water Authority awards an annual block permit to the Leeds Birdwatchers' Club. Eccup is a notable counting station. Large gull roost. Winter ducks include the Goosander. Plantations nearby hold a varied stock of woodland species.

SE 470278 **Fairburn Ings:** Close to the Great North Road just north of Ferrybridge. Reserve of 618 acres (200 being open water) since 1957. Now under the management of the R.S.P.B. and, with a full time warden, the area is owned by the National Coal Board. A raised public footpath crosses the main area of water. Fairburn's present marshland and open water dates from subsidence associated with mining and is frequented by a rich and diverse bird life, over 200 species having been noted. Breeding species of duck are Mallard, Teal, Gadwall, Shoveler, Tufted, Pochard. Breeding waders: Lapwing, Snipe, Little Ringed Plover, Redshank. The Great Crested and Little Grebe breed regularly. Many passage waders in spring and autumn. Visitors in early May following east winds are Black Tern, Spoonbill and Little Gull. Vast roosting flocks of Sand Martins (July/September), and Swallows (August/October). Numbers of Starlings and Yellow Wagtails roost in the reed-beds with hirundines. Winter visitors can include: divers, Goldeneye, Whooper and Bewick's Swans. A road runs along the northern edge of the reserve and many of its birds can be seen without leaving the roadway. For more details consult *"Fairburn and its Nature Reserve" (Dalesman* Mini-books).

TA 125808 **Filey Brigg:** On the Yorkshire coast, just north of the resort of Filey. Ample parking space on cliff-top just above the Brigg, which is a promontory of rock extending far out to sea. Good vantage point at passage and "fall" times and also to observe seabird movements at all times. One of the few Yorkshire sites where Purple Sandpipers are regular in winter. Red-breasted Merganser and Eider are often seen in winter, when a visit can also be rewarded by the sighting of Long-tailed Duck. The clifftop may hold Shorelark and Snow and Lapland Buntings in late autumn and winter.

TA 257706 **Flamborough Head:** Just north of Bridlington, on the Yorkshire coast. Final flourish of the chalk wolds with near vertical cliffs overtopped thickly with boulder clay. Extreme care should be used when visiting the cliffs. Besides being a good area in which to see considerable numbers of auks, Kittiwakes and Fulmars, Flamborough is a landfall for many North Sea migrants and a vantage point from which to observe a sea passage of terns, Skuas and Shearwaters.

SE 032317 **Fly Flatts Reservoir:** High Pennine reservoir south of Haworth and Oxenhope. Overland passage waders. Moorland species in surrounding areas.

TA 984873 **Forge Valley, Scarborough:** Adjacent to the well-known resort. Frequented by Nuthatch, Redstart, Great Spotted Woodpecker, Turtle Dove, Dipper; a stronghold of the Wood Warbler. Regular feeding at layby has encouraged remarkable tameness among Blackbird, Chaffinch, Robin, Nuthatch, tits and woodpeckers.

SE 125698 **Gouthwaite Reservoir:** Upper Nidderdale, between Pateley Bridge and Ramsgill. Site of glacial lake, re-flooded by Bradford Corporation as a compensation water when the big reservoirs were created at the dalehead. Now owned by the Yorkshire Water Authority. The road west of the water offers good viewing conditions. Gouthwaite is attractive to a variety of birds especially at its shallow upper end. Nesting by several pairs of Canada Geese, but at peak times there can be 140 or more Canadas present. Breeding by Tufted Duck. In winter, flock of between 30 and 50 Curlew; also a big gull roost (mostly of Black-headed but with Common Gulls numerically strong), and assemblies of Mallard, Wigeon and Teal. Also present in winter are Pochard, Goldeneye, Goosander and, rarely, the Smew. Herons in good numbers. Great Grey Shrike, Buzzard and harriers also occur.

SD 989649 **Grass Woods:** Upper Wharfedale, a little up-dale from Grassington. A representative collection of deciduous-woodland-nesting birds, including Nuthatch and woodpeckers, with birds coming readily to regular feeding areas.

SE 060645 **Grimwith Reservoir:** Moorland situation not far from the high road between Grassington (Wharfedale) and Pateley Bridge (Nidderdale). Controlled by the Yorkshire Water Authority. Grimwith, in its fine moorland setting, attracts a variety of water birds. Substantial breeding colony of Canada Geese, also Wigeon and Ringed Plover observed.

SE 312443 **Harewood Park and Bird Garden:** Beside the A61 where it is crossed by the A659 between Harrogate and Leeds. Bird garden of about 4 acres on a southward slope between the stables and Harewood Lake, contains some 600 birds of 150 species, ranging in size from Emu (the second largest bird in the world) to Hummingbird (the smallest). The majority of these birds are kept in outside aviaries or are at liberty in the garden. Bridle paths through parts of the estate woodlands can be used by visitors, providing they stay on the paths. The Lake, some 30 acres in extent, is a popular area for our own waterfowl, also a large flock of Canada Geese. Other species seen here: Great Crested Grebe, Tufted Duck, Pochard, Teal, Shoveler and, at times, Whooper Swan. British species to be seen within the Bird Garden include tits, Nuthatch, Tree-creeper, various finches and Collared Dove. In the winter of 1975-76, a female Long-tailed Duck was seen, and later an Osprey stayed in the area for a short period. The owners erected a lakeside hide for birdwatchers in 1976; the key to it is available on request.

TA 006971 **Hayburn Wyke:** On the Yorkshire coast, between Scarborough and Robin Hood's Bay. Reserve of 34 acres leased from the Forestry Commission by the Yorkshire Naturalists' Trust. About 40 species of birds recorded. Pied Flycatcher, Redstart and Blackcap, Treecreeper and Great Spotted Woodpecker nest.

TA 190470 **Hornsea Mere:** On the Yorkshire coast, at the edge of the town after which it is named. The Mere, an R.S.P.B. reserve, is the largest natural freshwater lake in Yorkshire, almost 1½ miles long and over 300 acres in extent. The reserve also covers a surrounding area of agricultural land, reed-swamp and woodland, bringing the total area under supervision to 580 acres. The only access is along the public footpath on the south side of the Mere. This path is not along the water's edge, but from it quite good views of the birds can be enjoyed. Rowing boats may be hired at Kirkholme Point from Hornsea Mere Marine Company; non-boating areas, providing refuges, are the bay north of Kirkholme Point and the western end. The warden organises escorted walks at prescribed times without prior arrangement; details from the warden enclosing, out of courtesy, a stamped envelope. The main importance of the Mere is a winter refuge for waterfowl and as a breeding place for large numbers of Reed Warblers. Breeding birds include Mallard, Gadwall, Tufted Duck, Pochard, Canada and Greylag Goose, Great Crested Grebe, Coot, Sedge Warbler and Reed Bunting. Winter duck numbers can be large, with most of the common species represented. Hornsea Mere is famous for the large number of wintering Goldeneye it attracts. Of the rarer reed-bed birds we might mention Bittern and Bearded Tit, which sometimes occur in autumn and winter; and Marsh Harrier, in spring. Hornsea Mere is of importance to many passage migrants requiring freshwater habitats and there is a tree roost of Cormorants.

SE 880250 **Humber Wildfowl Refuge:** This was established in the estuary and west of Hull to preserve the roosting area of wintering Pink-footed Geese. Many ducks may be seen, including Mallard, Teal and Wigeon. Shelduck are general in the area. Waders use the mud at low tide.

SD 705745 **Ingleton Falls:** A walk on hard paths and bridges from the village on the A65. Common Sandpiper, Grey Wagtail and Dipper are seen along the streams. Curlews, Lapwings and some other waders are abundant in nearby areas.

SE 228459 **Knotford Nook:** In the Wharfe Valley below Otley. Flooded gravel-pits attract Canada Geese, often in high numbers. Duck species include Goldeneye and occasionally Smew. Kingfishers are often seen. The ranks of gulls are worth scanning for the possibility of seeing a Glaucous Gull.

SK 192865 **Ladybower and Derwent Reservoirs:** On the county boundary with Derbyshire, they attract ducks and waders. The Common Sandpiper is seen in summer. The surrounding area, being well-wooded, increases the range of bird species to be seen. The Woodcock is present, also Redpoll, Spotted Flycatcher and Cuckoo. Hawks and owls should be looked for.

SE 213004 **Langsett and Broomhead Reservoirs:** West of Sheffield. They are close to and in some respects similar to Ladybower and Derwent, but they lie in a more open and less well-wooded area. Rough-legged Buzzards have sometimes been recorded in winter.

SE 157787 **Leighton Reservoir:** Near Masham. Canada Geese are frequently seen; some pairs breed on surrounding moorland. Leighton has a large gull roost. Ducks are plentiful in winter, and the Goosander is a regular species.

SD 800785 **Ling Gill:** In North Ribblesdale, fairly close to Ribblehead. Administered by the Nature Conservancy Council (Merlewood, Grange-over-Sands), from whom a permit to visit must be obtained. Ling Gill is a small wooded ravine in the limestone at about 1,000 feet above sea level. Much indigenous vegetation survives because of partial protection from grazing by sheep. Typical gill-frequenting bird species: Great Spotted Woodpecker, Wren, Dipper, Ring Ouzel, Blackbird, Redstart, Grey Wagtail, with Pied and Yellow Wagtail and Wheatear to be found nearby.

SD 895667 **Malham Tarn:** On Malham Moor, approached from Arncliffe, Langcliffe or Malham. The Tarn extends to 153 acres and was one of the first areas in the country to be designated an S.S.S.I. Though in Limestone Craven, water has gathered on Silurian rock at 1,230 feet above sea level. Adjacent mossland extends to about 88 acres. Malham Tarn is a field study centre, on lease from the National Trust. A footpath runs east of the water, passing the rear of the house. The Tarn is a nesting place for several pairs of Great Crested Grebe. Tufted Duck also breed, the first record of successful nesting being made in 1907. Small numbers of breeding Shoveler, but flocks of up to 50 Shoveler are seen in autumn. Woodland species present: Nuthatch, Great Spotted Woodpecker, Redpoll, Marsh Tit, Redstart, Spotted Flycatcher. Secondary growth is scarce, and most of the Song Thrushes nest on the ground. The Tarn is a gull roost, patronised mainly by Black-headed Gulls, whose numbers peak at between 10,000 and 12,000. On nearby Fountains Fell, the highest part of the parish of Malham Moor, Golden Plover, Dunlin and Red Grouse nest. The Pennine Way crosses this fell.

SE 403276 **Mickletown Flash:** Near Castleford. An area of subsidence, with a variety of breeding and visiting birds very similar to those encountered at Fairburn Ings. Mickleton is, incidentally, of equal interest for botanists and entomologists.

SE 856874 **North Yorkshire Forests:** Coniferous forest, most of it owned by the Forestry Commission, covers a good deal of the southern edge of the North York Moors. The public may walk almost anywhere to follow quiet recreational pursuits. Pickering Forest District (over 30,000 acres) is the largest forest tract on upland heath in England. The plantations extend mainly in large, adjacent blocks within a 20 mile radius of Scarborough, with outliers towards the Esk Valley (in the north) and on the chalk wolds beyond the Vale of Pickering (to the south). Most of the Forest lies within the North York Moors National Park. A visitor's map is available. Among the bird species to be seen are: Nightjar, Jay, Great Spotted Woodpecker, Tree Pipit, Sparrowhawk, Crossbill, Siskin, Redpoll, Goldcrest, with Short-eared Owl and harriers in the newer plantations.

TA 334185 **Patrington Haven:** On Humber shore. Large numbers of waders under right tidal conditions. Drainage channels in the area may present Sandpipers, including Common and Green, also Greenshank. Possibility of Marsh Harriers on migration over salt marsh areas. Shelduck common.

SE 598007 **Potteric Carr:** Also known as Low Ellers. On the outskirts of Doncaster. A reserve of the Yorkshire Naturalists' Trust. A combination of poor drainage and mining subsidence has restored to carr-like conditions an area which was never successfully drained to make it of full agricultural value. Potteric Carr was formerly a celebrated fowling area, the first duck decoy in Britain being constructed here in 1657. This vast area of reed-fen is dissected by several railway embankments and was at one time threatened by a suggested route for the M18 motorway. Black-headed Gulls nest, and the nesting ducks are Tufted, Shoveler and Pochard. Common warblers are the Reed and Sedge. A wide variety of waders has been recorded. Species seen at Potteric include Kingfisher, Bittern, Marsh Harrier and Crane. Extensive work by local volunteers has improved both the habitat for birds and the facilities for observers.

SD 814595 **Ribble Valley:** Between Settle and Long Preston. Nesting in the area are Curlew, Lapwing, Oystercatcher, Redshank, Snipe, Mallard, Teal, with a few colonies of Sand Martins. The valley is now best known for the flocking of waders in late summer and autumn. Bird numbers can rise to around 2,000 each of Lapwing, Golden Plover and Curlew. In early spring, many of the Golden Plover—on attaining breeding dress for the nesting season—are revealed to be birds of the northern race. Floodwater in winter attracts a few Whooper and Bewick's Swans. Appreciable numbers of Wigeon and Teal. The Green Sandpiper has occasionally overwintered. The valley is on a main migration route. Birds recorded on passage include Ruff, Little Stint, Greenshank, Black-tailed Godwit and, outstandingly, two American waders: a Pectoral Sandpiper and Dowitcher.

SE 057438 **Riddlesden Low Wood:** Near Keighley. Ten acres of woodland leased from the Borough by the Yorkshire Naturalists' Trust. Nest-box scheme is encouraging bird diversity. Present are: Great and Lesser Spotted Woodpeckers, Redstart, Spotted Flycatcher, Wood and Willow Warbler, Chiffchaff and Tawny Owl.

SE 578849 **Rievaulx:** Near Helmsley. Here and at nearby Dun-combe Park are woodland birds in number and variety. They include the Nuthatch and Hawfinch.

SE 776247 **Saltmarshe Delph:** A reserve of the Yorkshire Naturalists' Trust. A public hide has been erected over a pool on and around which might be seen Pochard, Reed and Sedge Warblers. The Bearded Tit has been observed. Breeding in the area are Tree-creeper, Spotted Flycatcher, Blackcap and Gold-finch.

NZ 745128 **Scaling Dam:** Bordered by the Guisborough to Whitby road. This reservoir is widely used for sailing but does attract many birds. Among the waders recorded are Temminck's Stint, Terek Sandpiper and Wilson's Phalarope. The Great White Heron has been seen. In winter, Scaling Dam has a substantial gull roost.

SE 047157 **Scammonden Valley:** Beside the M62 west of Huddersfield. Sailing activities restrict the nesting water birds but passage migrants are interesting, and the surrounding area holds much of interest, the breeding species including Golden Plover, Red Grouse, Curlew, Whinchat and Twite.

SD 922878 **Semerwater:** Near Bainbridge, in Upper Wensley-dale. This natural lake in a glaciated side-valley has a relatively high nutrient content and supports a phytoplankton charac-teristic of rich waters. The lake is noted for its large number of species of mayfly, which are seen in flight towards the end of May and into June, and a good hatch draws scores of gulls. Boating takes place from May to October; in the off-season the visiting birds include a herd of Whooper Swans. The Short-eared Owl frequents newly afforested fell country round about.

SE 642374 **Skipwith Common:** North-east of Selby. A reserve of the Yorkshire Naturalists' Trust. Flat heathland, with pools, the common has Black-headed Gull colonies, breeding ducks and wintering wildfowl. Long-eared Owl, Grasshopper Warbler and Nightjar are specialities, but the casual visitor may be more impressed by the numbers of Redpolls and Long-tailed Tits. Regular "roding" by Woodcock in spring and summer in late evening. Three species of woodpecker occur. The number of species of bird recorded is over 130, of which 90 breed regularly.

SE 653195 **Southfield Reservoir:** Six miles south of Goole. The water is widely used for sailing, but ducks seen in recent years include Scaup and Long-tailed. A Slavonian Grebe was seen in February 1972.

47

TA 417151 **Spurn Peninsula:** At the mouth of the Humber, Spurn is a reserve of the Yorkshire Naturalists' Trust. A bird observatory run by the ornithological section of the Yorkshire Naturalists' Union has been established on this sand spit since 1946. The peninsula funnels birds passing down the East Coast or along the Humber into a narrow flight-line and provides one of the most spectacular places in Britain for observing migration. It is probably the best and most watched area in the county. Little Tern and Ringed Plover formerly nested in some numbers, but the latter are now a small remnant and the former have not nested successfully for some years. The widespread marram grass and sea buckthorn are used as nest sites by Linnet, Reed Bunting and Sedge Warbler. Tree Sparrows frequent the hollow concrete blocks from which some walls are constructed. Autumn brings a large-scale immigration of Fieldfares, Redwings, Blackbirds, Robins, Goldcrests and Woodcock from the Continent and Scandinavia. Rare species can be comparatively regular at Spurn and include: Bluethroat, Red-backed Shrike, Icterine Warbler and Wryneck, followed later in the autumn by Great Grey Shrike, Red-breasted Flycatcher, Pallas's Warbler and Yellow-browed Warbler. Spurn is a vantage point from which to see a good passage of seabirds. A regular autumn sight is that of skuas in pursuit of terns. In winter, Snow Buntings and Shore Larks occur and, in some years, there are rafts of Scaup. Brent Geese are present in small numbers. Winter flocks of Mallard and Wigeon can sometimes be impressive. The list of rarities which have occurred at Spurn is far too long to include. The observatory issues an annual report which should be consulted by would-be visitors.

SE 350238 **Stanley Sewage Farm:** Near Wakefield. Lying in a loop of the Calder, the sewage farm attracts gulls, Snipe, etc. Interesting waders may be viewed during periods of migration. The Spotted Crake has been seen. The area is virtually connected with Bottomboat and the Altofts Ings complex. Bottomboat is now less important ornithologically as a result of colliery tipping. Altofts is crossed by the M62 motorway.

SD 737562 **Stocks Reservoir:** Upper Hodder Valley, in Bowland. The reservoir, of 344 acres, has a small island, the nesting place of several thousand pairs of Black-headed Gulls, whose activities can be clearly seen through binoculars from a road running to the east of the water, between Slaidburn and Bowland Knotts. A pole was optimistically reared on the island to attract Osprey to nest (the species is seen with some regularity at passage time), but is used instead as a perch by Cormorants. Black Terns have several times been seen in spring; autumn

An immature Gannet. The chalk cliffs of Bempton hold the only gannetry on the English mainland.

Seal Sands, at the mouth of the Tees, where birds co-exist with heavy industry.

Right: Chalk Cliffs at Bempton, nesting place of Auks and Kittiwakes.

Below: Guillemots and Razorbills at Bempton.

The Derwent Valley below York, showing the lush summertime reed-growth.

Canada Geese and Mute Swans at Fairburn Ings, where colliery subsidence led to flooding.

Mute Swans nesting beside Hornsea Mere, which is the largest freshwater lake in Yorkshire.

Foresters' houses near the conifer plantations at Langdale, near Scarborough.

A Short-eared Owl at the nest. This species can be locally common in areas newly-planted with conifers.

Left: Twite, which nests where the ground vegetation is dense on parts of the southern Pennines.

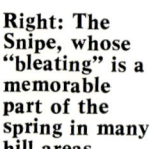

Right: The Snipe, whose "bleating" is a memorable part of the spring in many hill areas.

The Curlew, quite common nesting species in the west, where many pairs
now breed in low-lying meadows.

This Tree Pipit was host to a Cuckoo at a nest made in south-west Yorkshire.

Golden Plover, the "Pennine whistler", inhabits many tracts of high ground. Large wintering flocks are noted in some lowland situations.

occurrences of Ringed Plover and Greenshank, with much wader activity on what is a notable trans-Pennine migration route. Canada Geese nest in the area and outside the breeding season a flock of up to 70 Canadas with some Greylags might be seen. In winter, Stocks has a considerable gull roost. Wintering ducks include Goosander, and the number of these builds up to a figure in excess of 60 in March. A permit is needed for birdwatching other than from the public roads, also in the adjacent 3,000-acre Gisburn Forest (Forestry Commission).

SE 647615 **Strensall Common:** Near Strensall village, 6 miles north of York. A reserve of the Yorkshire Naturalists' Trust. The common, one of the few remaining lowland heaths in the Vale of York, has a stock of typical heathland birds, including the Nightjar. The Curlew also nests here.

SE 273683 **Studley Park:** Adjacent to Fountains Abbey, near Ripon. Owned by the North Yorkshire County Council. The Park is best-known for its deer (red, fallow, sika) but has a large lake with nesting Great Crested Grebe, Little Grebe and Common Sandpiper. Canada Geese have also nested by the lake but this species is more prominent after the moult when birds roost on the lake during the day and feed on stubbles during clear nights. Breeding species at Studley include: Tawny, Barn and Little Owls; Nuthatch, Great Spotted, Lesser Spotted and Green Woodpeckers. Birds of the river Skell include Kingfisher, Dipper and Grey Wagtail. A local celebrity is the Hawfinch. Yellow Wagtails are seen on passage during mid-May.

SE 388287 **Swillington Ings:** South-east of Leeds. A mining subsidence area, these Ings attract large numbers of migrant waders. The first-known breeding of Little Ringed Plover in Yorkshire occurred here in 1947. Temminck's Stint nested here in 1951, the first record for England. Great Crested and Little Grebes are regular visitors, with Black-necked and Slavonian Grebes frequently seen. Wintering species have included Whooper and Bewick's Swans, Goldeneye and Smew.

NY 897068 **Tan Hill:** Can be approached by road from Keld in Swaledale, Arkengarthdale or Barras near Brough. The whole of this area, "Kearton country", around the highest inn to be found in Britain, contains a wealth of moorland birds. The Pennine Way runs across the moor from Keld parallel to West Stonesdale, and it passes within a few yards of the inn before forging on to Stainmore. Colonies of Black-headed and Lesser Black-backed Gulls occur here. Grouse—both Red and Black—can be seen. Golden Plover, Lapwing and Curlew nest within sight of the road.

Redshank and Snipe are commonly seen perched on posts and walls. Dipper and Common Sandpiper frequent the streams. Song birds are few; the most common are Meadow Pipit, Wheatear and Skylark. Kestrels and Short-eared Owls may be seen quartering the moorland areas and the adjacent Barras Forest (in Cumbria). A birdwatcher is occasionally rewarded by the sight of a Merlin.

NZ 557277 **Teesmouth:** An estuary separating Yorkshire from County Durham. Teesmouth has been famed for its birds since before the time of Nelson, who wrote the two-volume work on Yorkshire birds. Despite industrial encroachment, vast numbers of waders use the area, including some Purple Sandpipers. A notable feature of Teesmouth is the autumn passage of skuas— e.g. 11 Great Skuas on September 17, 1972, and 20 Pomarine Skuas on October 11, 1972. Visitors in winter include Snow Bunting and Shore Lark. Red-breasted Merganser, Long-tailed Duck, Eider and sometimes Little Auk are seen. Oystercatchers and Shelduck can be numerous. As with Spurn and the Humber estuary, a complete list would be too extensive to include here; local reports should be consulted.

SE 711161 **Thorne Moors:** Part of the former extensive and important carr-land comprising Misterton Carr, Hatfield Chase, Thorne Waste and Goole Fields, which extended continuously from east of Bawtry and Doncaster to Goole. Large tracts remain undrained and uncultivated but have been ravaged in many places for the extraction of peat. Rapid re-colonisation of such areas by silver birch provides a healthy population of Redpolls, Whinchats and woodpeckers. Thorne holds a large colony of Black-headed Gulls, and ducks of various species breed. Some parts of the Moor are frequented by the Nightingale. Sedge and Reed Warblers are common in summer. Wheatears and Yellow and Pied Wagtails perch on peat stacks. Occasional winter visitors are Hen Harriers and Rough-legged Buzzards. So vast an area is Thorne Moor that a visitor has the false impression that there are not as many birds and species as do, in fact, occur. Over 140 species of birds have been observed, of which 70 have been found breeding.

SD 741746 **Three Peaks:** They are Whernside (2,414 feet), Ingleborough (2,373 feet) and Penyghent (2,273 feet), in northwest Yorkshire. The peaks are of Carboniferous stratum—limestone, Yoredale Series and with a capping of millstone grit. The number of nesting species is comparatively few, including Golden Plover, a few Dunlin, Short-eared Owl, Red Grouse, Curlew, Redshank, Lapwing, Snipe, Wheatear, Skylark and Meadow

Pipit. There are Dippers on the streams and Ring Ouzels in some of the gills. Ravens have nested; vagrant Buzzards are reported. Dotterel sometimes appear on Ingleborough during the spring migration to their more northerly breeding grounds. Snow Buntings feed on mollinia around the summit of this fell in most winters, and November is a good time to look for them.

TA 075490 **Tophill Low Reservoir:** In the valley of the river Hull east of the Beverley to Driffield road. 7 miles north-east of Beverley and near to the site of the ancient Watton decoy. Owned by the eastern division of the Yorkshire Water Authority, Tophill Low attracts large numbers of ducks, for example 400 Tufted in December; 130 Goldeneye in February and 26 Pintail in December, during the winter of 1972/3. In December 1973, 28 Goosanders were present.

SK 476960 **Thrybergh Reservoir:** Between Rotherham and Conisbrough. Owned by the Yorkshire Water Authority. Birdwatching by permit only. Wildfowl counts are made weekly throughout the winter.

SE 188542 **Washburn Valley:** Extends from the hill country near Greenhow, which is traversed by the B6265, to the market town of Otley, and includes 4 large reservoirs which can be scanned from public roads. The high ground holds typical nesting species such as Red Grouse, Curlew, Skylark, Meadow Pipit and Wheatear; with Ring Ouzels in the gills and Dippers on the streams. The reservoirs of Thruscross, Fewston, Swinsty and Lindley Wood are important areas for wildfowl. The nesting species include Canada Goose and Great Crested Grebe. In winter, Whooper Swans—less frequently, Bewick's Swans—can be seen, and Canada Geese can be present in large numbers, along with assemblies of duck. In lower Washburn, where the landscape is well-wooded, three species of woodpecker occur, together with Tawny, Barn and Little Owls. There is also a varied assembly of warblers — among them Sedge Warblers — together with Redstart, Spotted and Pied Flycatchers. Buzzards are not infrequently seen.

SE 428025 **Wath Ings:** In the Dearne Valley. Managed by the Yorkshire Naturalists' Trust under an agreement with the Yorkshire Water Authority. Areas of marshland and open water are good places in which to look for migrant waders and vagrant species, which have included Gannet and Glossy Ibis. Over 150 species of bird have been reported. Nesting wildfowl include the Shoveler. Wintering Short-eared Owls, Whooper and Bewick's Swans.

SE 698428 **Wheldrake Ings:** Valley of the Derwent, south-east of York. A reserve of the Yorkshire Naturalists' Trust. Resident warden. When the meadows flood—usually in December and January—large numbers of wildfowl are attracted. Whooper and Bewick's Swans are present; over 90 Bewick's were seen early in 1975. Large numbers of Mallard, Wigeon and Teal are attracted by the standing water. Short-eared Owls and Hen Harriers may be seen quartering the rough ground. When the floods recede there is still a convoluted pool with eight islands attractive to waders, sightings including Wood Sandpiper, Whimbrel, Spotted Redshank, Black-tailed Godwit and Ruff. Access to the reserve is by two bridges, a wooden bridge existing at West Cottingwith. Bird life can be seen from the banks of the Derwent, and a hide is provided.

SE 373152 **Wintersett Reservoir:** South-west of Wakefield, adjoining Haw Park (afforested area) and Walton Park, the former home of Charles Waterton. Good area for water birds and passing waders. Species seen include Black Tern, Sabine's Gull, Red-necked Grebe and divers. Haw Park has the usual woodland species, with a roost of Long-eared Owls reported from time to time. Walton Park can still be rewarding despite the greater disturbance as compared to the days when Waterton made it into the first bird sanctuary.

Bird Migration

SINCE a Yorkshireman, Eagle Clarke, produced *Studies in Bird Migration* in 1912, many experiments and reports, articles and even whole books have contributed fresh facts and theories, evidence and conjecture. Obviously the subject is so fascinating and complex that it is impossible to cover it comprehensively here. Rather, we can perhaps look at certain facets as they have been and can be observed in Yorkshire. Perhaps the simplest way of doing this is to follow changes in populations during the course of a year.

We may already have noticed that some species of birds had arrived to spend the winter in this country. Fieldfares and Redwings are obviously winter visitors. Because species like Black-headed Gull, Tufted Duck and Starling are with us all the year round, we may not have appreciated that many of the individuals which we see in winter are in fact immigrant birds from further north and east. Ringing has shown that some Black-headed Gulls, found in Yorkshire in winter, have come from Baltic countries. Starlings have originated from Poland and Russia; while a Tufted Duck ringed as a nestling in Finland in June was found in Yorkshire in a subsequent January, and a Wigeon shot near Selby in February was of Icelandic breeding stock.

Fieldfares and Redwings move about the countryside in flocks, stripping hedgerows of their berries, and later dropping into the fields where they become ground-feeders. A spell of frost and snow in the early part of the year obviously denies ground-feeders their livelihood. Should it be prolonged and widespread, it may result in many deaths. Its onset will trigger off one kind of easily observable migration known as a hard-weather movement, when birds seek areas where food is still accessible. Lapwings and Skylarks are among the most prominent species in these hard-weather movements, but Fieldfares and Redwings may also disappear temporarily from our locality or a few will lose their shyness and come to gardens where resident species have learned to expect food.

As winter conditions begin to relax, and daylight to lengthen, we notice an increase in the numbers of some species of ducks and an air of restlessness in their behaviour. Goldeneye and Smew may reach their peak numbers in February and March, though it is as well to remind ourselves that no two seasons are predictably and exactly alike. These ducks are among the earliest to head northwards. Goldeneye may be seen in full display on many of our lakes and reservoirs although they may still have several hundred miles to travel before they finally nest in a hole in a tree, perhaps in Scandinavia.

Reservoirs around London hold good numbers of Smew in winter, and large numbers of Bewick's Swans congregate in the Severn estuary. As these swans start their return journey to Siberia they may well find February flooding at Wheldrake and Bubwith Ings. If they do, they will linger in Yorkshire for a week or two on one stage of their migration. Whooper Swans tend to stay longer with us but numbers gradually decline from mid-March.

In the meantime, an increase is discernible in the numbers of wading birds on moorland breeding grounds, well before winter has had its final fling. Though Redshank, Lapwing, Curlew and Golden Plover may move only from the high moors to the lowlands or the coast in autumn, and return again in early spring, this too is a limited form of migration (sometimes referred to as vertical migration). Watchers in lowland areas often record the movements of these birds, and of Oystercatchers and Meadow Pipits in March.

By the end of the month, we begin to look for the first returning summer visitors from overseas—Chiffchaff, Sand Martin, Ring Ouzel and Wheatear. This last species may already have been on Pennine breeding grounds for a week or two before lowland watchers see Wheatears on arable land and spoil-heaps. These later birds are undoubtedly on their way further north, to Iceland and Greenland for instance. Chaffinches can be seen passing along Spurn peninsula in late March, often in considerable numbers, reminding us yet again that the populations of what we regard as resident species are not static. We receive additional birds in winter from further north; some which have bred here move south and west. We have already noted that some of our wintering Black-headed Gulls have arrived from Baltic countries; some of those ringed here in the breeding season move out to Ireland in the winter. Birds like Redpolls and Meadow Pipits can be seen at all seasons, but some ringed here are reported later from Belgium or the Biscay area.

At the same time that the Chaffinches are seen in numbers on the coast (visible migration) easterly winds will bring Black Redstarts and Goldcrests (drift migrants).

The flood of spring migration really gets under way by mid-April and is marked for the average person by his first sighting of a Swallow or by the first Cuckoo's call, the latter not usually until the third week in April. In early May some of the later summer visitors arrive, and among them are the Spotted Fly-catcher and Turtle Dove. How short a proportion of the year some of them spend in their breeding areas can be appreciated when we realise that the majority of Swifts do not reach us until the first week of May and most have disappeared by the third in August.

This aspect is even more remarkable when we consider the wading birds which nest in Arctic regions. Early May is the time when birdwatchers are on the alert for these passage waders. Unless one is fortunate enough to be able to visit their breeding grounds in the far north, this is the only opportunity to see some of them in their attractive breeding plumage. Ruff, Spotted Redshank and Wood Sandpiper may be expected. The Black-tailed Godwits which we sometimes see in May are probably Icelandic birds rather than a part of the re-established British breeding stock. The earliest wading birds on the return passage southwards may be seen in July, and they are possibly individuals which have failed to find a mate or whose nesting attempts in the uncertain conditions of the Arctic have been unsuccessful. Sometimes only one of the pair remains in the far north to tend the young, which must start the long journey south almost as soon as they are able to fly.

In addition to the waders, May can provide us with sightings of birds like Marsh Harrier and Osprey, possibly birds which are not fully mature and so do not feel the same urgency to reach recognised breeding areas. Easterly winds bring other drift-migrants in May. Black Tern and Little Gull often occur together, and under similar conditions a Spoonbill may be seen. Other terns pass through inland areas as well as along the coast.

The tides of migration of one sort or another are never still. The large assemblies of Swifts which one encounters at places like Knostrop and Fairburn in high summer, when there is a hatch of insects, must have congregated from a wide area. Their "following food" can be regarded as a form of temporary and local migration. High summer may also produce evidence of migration of a further kind. A high population of Crossbills, resulting from a series of good breeding seasons, sometimes coincides with a shortage of their particular requirement in food. There is then a mass exodus of these birds from north-east Europe and we periodically get what is known as a Crossbill "invasion". This species may arrive in June or July, spreading from the east coast to inland conifer plantations in search of pine seeds. With increased afforestation a few pairs may remain in Yorkshire to breed in the following season. The same sort of causes are behind the "eruptive" movements of Bearded Tits in autumn, or influxes of Waxwings or Nutcrackers. In earlier years, Pallas's Sand Grouse behaved in a similar way.

The Crossbills are not the only birds moving in July. Moult migration is the explanation of the Shelducks we see inland during this month. They are making their way across from the west coast towards the Heligoland Bight where they spend their flightless moult period. Common Scoters are moving between east and western seaboards at the same time and may alight for a time on inland reservoirs. Most of the Yorkshire Canada Geese move northwards to moult, heading for Beauly Firth. Lapwings begin to gather into large flocks in late summer in many parts of the county; and the large numbers of Curlew which congregate at Malham, Stocks Reservoir and in the Ribble Valley, are heard calling a great deal and display "migratory restlessness".

In late summer, flocks of terns and Kittiwakes assemble at points on the coast. They spend a considerable time lazing on the shore but disperse, to the accompaniment of the terns' raucous calls, as soon as an Arctic Skua comes on the scene. There are few more fascinating things to watch in the bird world than the piratical attacks of the skuas on migrating terns and Kittiwakes, with Teesmouth as a good vantage point. As Swallows and Martins begin their long journey back—for many of them that journey leads to South Africa — they begin to gather in flocks on rooftops and wires. They often roost in large numbers in reedbeds as they move steadily southwards.

When we see Willow Warblers picking greedily from our roses in the garden in August, we are observing a small part of a migratory movement. More spectacular evidence is often obtained by going to the coast and seeing scores of Wheatears, Whinchats, Redstarts and Pied Flycatchers. Further into autumn, Robins and Goldcrests arrive. Not infrequently there is a sprinkling of rare birds such as Bluethroat, Icterine and Barred Warblers, Wryneck and Red-backed Shrike.

Obviously more birds are involved in the autumn migration, since the season's young add to the total. How chancy the breeding by birds can be in the far north is underlined by the differences between one year and another in the proportion of these young birds.

September is the best month for seeing many of the waders. How much we see of them depends also on weather conditions and water-levels. During the following month a watcher at the coast (Spurn and Flamborough are two recognised vantage points) may see land birds arriving from over the sea. Movements of Fieldfares, Redwings, Blackbirds and Starlings are easy to identify. In late October, incoming flocks of Starlings sometimes "pick up" a stray Little Auk which heads inland with them, impelled by some flocking instinct. Larger birds like Short and Long-eared Owls and Woodcock are usually seen arriving singly.

A Check List

SPECIES of bird which a visitor to Yorkshire might see, given time and luck. This is not an exhaustive list and in the space available only a brief outline can be given. For more detailed information a reader should consult the definitive works, annual county ornithological reports and those of reserves and local societies. Also, recorders in local societies will be able to provide information about the possibility of seeing any bird species within their area, and will in their turn welcome observations.

BLACK-THROATED DIVER *(Gavia arctica)*
Seen on inland waters, infrequently, in winter. Birds in summer plumage have been observed by coastal watchers in spring. A Black-throat seen off Filey Brigg in October had the remnants of the summer plumage on its back.

GREAT NORTHERN DIVER *(Gavia immer)*
Seen occasionally in large coastal bays — e.g., Scarborough, Bridlington, Filey. Usually single birds. Not often observed on inland waters.

WHITE-BILLED DIVER *(Gavia Adamsii)*
Up to and including 1973, of the 39 birds of this species which occurred in Britain, nine were from Yorkshire. Two Yorkshire ornithologists, D. Burns and J. Mather of Knaresborough, have made a special study of the identification of this species which unfortunately is usually recorded only as a coastal casualty. All dead divers on the coast need to be examined carefully.

RED-THROATED DIVER *(Gavia stellata)*
The commonest of the wintering divers. Groups of over 100 birds observed at the coast January/March, up to 200 recorded on days of good passage. Occasional visitor to inland waters, usually in winter, but a bird in full breeding plumage was seen on Dale Dyke reservoir in July 1973.

GREAT CRESTED GREBE *(Podiceps cristatus)*
The nesting population at inland waters has been steadily increasing over the past half century, mostly on reed-edged lakes

at fairly low elevation. Among the many lowland haunts are Bretton and Newmillerdam, but nesting also occurs at Malham Tarn (c. 1,000 feet). This grebe may be seen in sheltered coastal areas in winter; it has overwintered on some inland lakes.

RED-NECKED GREBE *(Podiceps griseigena)*
As a winter visitor, this grebe is seen mainly on the coast, occasionally inland.

SLAVONIAN GREBE *(Podiceps auritus)*
The Slavonian Grebe, a winter visitor, has been recorded with some regularity at Hornsea Mere. Occasional visitor to many inland waters.

BLACK-NECKED GREBE *(Podiceps nigricollis)*
The Black-necked Grebe has been recorded more often than the Slavonian and has also nested in the county. Eight birds were seen together on Agden reservoir in October 1973.

LITTLE GREBE *(Tachybaptus ruficollis)*
Also known as dabchick. Most common and well-distributed of the nesting grebes. Flocking is a regular feature in August and September, when as many as 50 are often seen on a single water. Has been recorded at the coast in winter.

LEACH'S PETREL *(Oceanodroma leucorrhoa)*
Periodically "wrecks" of these sea-birds occur in autumn under adverse weather conditions and they are recorded from inland as well as coastal sites, mostly as casualties.

MANX SHEARWATER *(Puffinus puffinus)*
In late summer and early autumn, birds can be seen passing along the Yorkshire coast, well out at sea, with occasional Sooty Shearwaters, on the best days of sea passage. Occasional "wrecked" birds inland.

FULMAR *(Fulmarus glacialis)*
Nests on all suitable cliffs from Saltburn to Sewerby, also in a quarry near Guisborough. Breeding sites include Castle Hill, Scarborough, where in 1974 the number of pairs in occupation was 52. At this most easily observed nesting area, a few birds have been seen back on the ledges in late November.

GANNET *(Sula bassana)*
Growing nesting colony on the old Guillemot ledges of Jubilee Corner, Bempton, the only gannetry in England. The first successful nest here was seen in 1937, and the Gannet population rose slowly until the cessation of cliff-climmin' for the eggs of sea birds (1953). The gannetry has since increased considerably, with birds spreading from the original point of colonisation. A total of 103 Gannet chicks was noted in 1975. Two chicks died on becoming entangled in nylon fishing net the parents had collected as nesting material. A bird colour-ringed at Bass Rock, in

the Firth of Forth, has been seen at Bempton, hinting at the origin of the colonising stock. Adults and young disperse in September, but Gannets in flight can be seen off the coast throughout the year.

CORMORANT *(Phalacrocorax carbo)*
Nests on the northern part of the Yorkshire coast. Small colonies at Huntcliff, Ravenscar and Gristhorpe. The Cormorant is frequently seen off the coast outside the nesting season, a number of birds roosting on anti-submarine piles in the Humber. Inland lakes and reservoirs are visited, including Bretton Park lake, Stocks Reservoir in Bowland, the reservoirs at Wintersett, Chelker, Gouthwaite, also Semerwater and Fairburn Ings; with Hornsea Mere and Seamer Road Mere at Scarborough (nearer the coast). Tree-roosting has been noted at Hornsea, where over 50 birds were present at the year end in 1974, and where White-headed Cormorants, presumably of continental origin, have been observed.

SHAG *(Phalacrocorax aristotelis)*
Returned to Bempton in 1952 after a long absence, and there were 20 pairs in 1969. Off-season groups of birds in Filey Bay and at the Brigg, where 110 birds were logged in October 1974. The Shag favours ledges in caves. Periodically reported as a "wreck" species from inland waters after stormy weather in autumn and winter. Two Shags were shot in Pontefract Park in the winter of 1975/6, one of which had been ringed on the Isle of May.

GREY HERON *(Ardea cinerea)*
The nesting population is now believed to exceed 200. Heronries include Kirkby Fleetham, Healaugh near Tadcaster and near Coniston Cold, with new colonies located from time to time. A heronry of former times was by the lake in Harewood Park. Although most heronries are usually at low elevations, birds feed at upland reservoirs, lakes and fell streams. A dozen or more Herons may be seen feeding by the stream at the head of Gouthwaite Reservoir, in Nidderdale, in winter. A Swedish bird ringed in May 1973 was found injured in Leeds in the following September.

SPOONBILL *(Platalea leucorodia)*
A few recorded in most years, more particularly inland in spring after easterly winds.

BITTERN *(Botaurus stellaris)*
Recorded in most years, usually in winter, from a number of areas.

MALLARD *(Anas platyrhynchos)*
Widespread and common in the nesting season, and numbers

augmented by winter visitors from the continent. Breeds at over 1,000 feet on the Pennines. Day roosts in winter at Humber Wildfowl Refuge, Hornsea Mere, Fairburn Ings, also the reservoirs of Eccup and Leighton (up to 700 birds at the latter) and in the Masham area generally. Where wild stock is hand-reared —as at Clapham and some other Yorkshire villages—there is a risk of hybridisation with domestic strains of duck, notably the Aylesbury and Khaki Campbell.

TEAL *(Anas crecca)*
Breeds in moorland areas, including upper Nidderdale and North Craven as well as in lowland localities. Nest found at an elevation of 2,100 feet on Fountains Fell. As a winter visitor, the Teal is at peak numbers in Yorkshire from September and October. Wintering haunts include: Hornsea Mere, Lower Derwent floods, Fairburn Ings, Gouthwaite Reservoir, in the Birkin area east of Brotherton, and the Humber Wildfowl Refuge.

GARGANEY *(Anas querquedula)*
A small number of birds is reported occasionally from low-elevation waters in southern Yorkshire during the breeding season.

GADWALL *(Anas strepera)*
Numbers tend to be small except at Hornsea Mere and Fairburn, where between 100-140 and 50-60 respectively have been recorded. Now breeds sparingly in the county. Three Gadwall were seen on the lake at Butlin's camp, Filey, in January 1974.

WIGEON *(Anas penelope)*
Nests sparingly on moorland on n.w. Yorkshire. As a winter visitor, it is relatively common in the Tees and Humber estuaries and on the Derwent floods. Largest numbers, 2,000 plus at times in winter on Humber Wildfowl Refuge, and in the same season 2,000-3,000 under flood conditions in Lower Derwent Valley. An off-coast passage of Wigeon has been noted in September.

PINTAIL *(Anas acuta)*
The favoured haunts of this winter visitor are Lower Derwent floods, Humber Wildfowl Refuge, Hornsea Mere. Small numbers on many inland waters, though it is seldom that more than 20 are seen.

SHOVELER *(Anas clypeata)*
Nests at Fairburn Ings and several other sites in south Yorkshire; also at Gouthwaite in Nidderdale. More than 100 birds may be seen at peak times in spring and autumn—notably at Hornsea, Fairburn Ings, Potteric Carr.

SCAUP *(Aythya marila)*
Small numbers at many inland waters in most years. Periodically

a large flock (sometimes up to c. 400 birds) may be stationed at Spurn through the winter.

TUFTED DUCK *(Aythya fuligula)*

Nesting population increasing, a particularly high site being Malham Tarn, at over 1,000 feet (seven broods in 1973). The Tufted Duck also breeds at Hornsea Mere, Fairburn Ings, Swillington Ings, Potteric Carr, Gouthwaite Reservoir, Farnham G.P. and other waters. Autumnal build-up through immigration. Wintering haunts with large numbers include Hornsea Mere, Tophill Reservoir and Fairburn Ings. Ducklings ringed in Holland in 1969 were found dead at Hornsea in April 1970.

POCHARD *(Aythya ferina)*

Breeds in a few Yorkshire areas, notably Fairburn Ings, Swillington Ings, Hornsea Mere. Numbers augmented by winter visitors from eastern Europe from late September to April, when areas to watch include not only the above but also Lower Derwent floods, and many other waters. Coniston Cold lake held 300 plus in September 1973.

GOLDENEYE *(Bucephala clangula)*

This winter visitor may be seen from October until late May, by which time some birds are displaying. Occasional birds have been reported as early as June/July. The largest wintering groups are usually reported from Tophill Reservoir, Hornsea Mere, Gouthwaite, Cornelian Bay near Scarborough and Fairburn Ings. Numbers at Yorkshire haunts generally peak in March to mid-April, with occasionally up to 150 birds at Hornsea. The Goldeneye has summered at Gouthwaite and Knotford Nook.

LONG-TAILED DUCK *(Clangula hyemalis)*

Many sightings along the coast in winter with Bridlington Bay, Filey Brigg, Teesmouth (South Gare) as places to watch. Numbers of birds tend to be small. Some occasional inland occurrences.

COMMON SCOTER *(Melanitta nigra)*

Birds often seen out at sea, especially off Spurn, sometimes in considerable numbers and mainly in the latter half of the year. Marked passage overland from east to west coasts, especially in July when small parties may drop down to inland waters.

EIDER *(Somateria mollissima)*

A few birds may be seen off the coast throughout the year. Places to watch include: South Gare, Filey Brigg, Cornelian Bay near Scarborough and rocky stretches of coast between Bridlington and Flamborough. Occasional inland records.

RED-BREASTED MERGANSER *(Mergus serrator)*

Has bred successfully in recent years in the northern half of the county, including Upper Hodder Valley and Wensleydale. Outside the nesting season, birds are seen off the coast and on some inland waters.

GOOSANDER *(Mergus merganser)*
As a breeding species, the Goosander is in small numbers. Has nested by the Tees, Dee (Dentdale) and Wharfe. As a winter visitor, it occurs on several waters, including the reservoirs of Stocks, Leighton, Chelker, Gouthwaite, Washburndale. Tophill Low and Eccup. Also reported from Castle Howard, Fairburn Ings and Hornsea Mere. A flock of more than 50 is exceptional.

SMEW *(Mergus albellus)*
A species which appears in small numbers, more commonly in the later months of the winter, December to March. Most birds are the red-heads (female or young birds). The beautifully plumaged drake which gives the species the name "white nun" is less often seen.

SHELDUCK *(Tadorna tadorna)*
Nests by Yorkshire estuaries with some pairs inland as far from the coast as Swillington. Moult migration of west coast birds over the Pennines in late summer. At passage time, birds—usually singles—may be seen at various inland waters or overhead on their way to Heligoland Bight. Most numerous on coast in January/April, and September/December.

GREYLAG *(Anser anser)*
As a breeding species the Greylag is local. The situation is confused by feral birds. Small groups of Greylags tend to associate with Canada Geese at waters in central Yorkshire. A few Greylags moulted with a large flock of Canadas at Scar House Reservoir, upper Nidderdale. Resident flock at Hornsea Mere.

PINK-FOOTED GOOSE *(Anser brachyrhynchus)*
Generally a winter visitor, but single birds reported as associating with Canada Geese in summer. Maximum number of Pinkfeet counted at Humber Wildfowl Refuge in 1974 was 1,600 in October, a much lower figure than in earlier years. Another notable roost exists at the mouth of the Ribble estuary and skeins commuting between east and west coast are frequently seen by observers in west Yorkshire, especially in November and December.

CANADA GOOSE *(Branta canadensis)*
Nesting occurs in and around Wharfedale and Nidderdale, at Farnham Gravel Pits, Gouthwaite, Leighton Reservoir, Roundhill Reservoir, Ripley Park, Allerton Park, Sawley High Moor. Other waters of note: Fairburn, Harewood Park, Bretton Park (over 100 in mid-winter), Studley Park lake, Hornsea Mere. Autumn assemblies of over 500 birds in the Nidd Valley. Birds

ringed in Yorkshire in July have been re-trapped and controlled on the Beauly Firth, in north-east Scotland, where many go to moult. Moulting birds ringed at Beauly have been recorded back in Yorkshire during the breeding season. Colour-ringing in recent years has enabled watchers to establish the exchange of birds between areas.

MUTE SWAN *(Cygnus olor)*
Breeding species on many inland waters, including the Leeds and Liverpool canal at Skipton. Has also nested on the lake at Butlin's camp near Filey. Up to 200 assemble at Fairburn in summer for the moult period.

WHOOPER SWAN *(Cygnus cygnus)*
Icelandic-nesting birds arrive in late October, returning north in March to April. Single Whoopers, possibly injured birds, have occasionally summered in Yorkshire. In winter, Whooper Swans frequent Fairburn Ings, and other waters in the lower Aire Valley, Semerwater, Gouthwaite. Temporary floodwater is attractive, as in the Derwent Valley and in the Ribble Valley between Settle and Long Preston. Family ties are strong, and even when a herd of 40 or 50 birds has joined together the family groups can be distinguished. Young birds of the year stay very much with their parents. These swans are almost entirely vegetarian, feeding on the leaves and roots of water plants. Later in the winter they frequently graze on dry land.

BEWICK'S SWAN *(Cygnus bewickii)*
Birds seen in Yorkshire in winter come from north-east Russia, and the northern coasts of Siberia, arriving at the end of October and lingering until March or even early April. Generally fewer in number than the Whooper, the Bewick is also slightly smaller in size. Bewick's Swans have been reported from Fairburn Ings, Birkin, Hornsea Mere, Knotford Nook, Semerwater and a number of other inland waters. They are seen on floodwater, especially from January to March when they may be moving northwards from the Severn towards their breeding haunts. Two favoured areas are the Lower Derwent Valley and north Ribblesdale. Favourite estuarine haunts on the Humber are near Kilnsea and Paull.

GOLDEN EAGLE *(Aquila chrysaetos)*
A Golden Eagle was killed near Kilnsey in Wharfedale in 1902. There was then a long lapse before the species was again reported in Yorkshire. An immature bird seen at Gouthwaite, Nidderdale, in December and January 1970/71 was possibly a young bird from Lakeland.

BUZZARD *(Buteo buteo)*
A few pairs breed in north-west Yorkshire, but single birds—

71

including young of the year—are reported from several parts of the dales down to mid and lower Airedale in autumn and winter. The Buzzard has also been seen on the Southern Pennines.

ROUGH-LEGGED BUZZARD *(Buteo lagopus)*
A large autumnal influx of this winter visitor occurred in 1973, mainly in the north-east. A number of birds over-summered. Another influx was noted in the latter part of 1974.

SPARROWHAWK *(Accipiter nisus)*
Now breeding again generally throughout the county in small numbers after being almost wiped out during the last decade as a result of toxic chemicals picked up from prey species. New conifer forests—and especially larch plantations within them—are now much-used nesting sites.

MARSH HARRIER *(Circus aeruginosus)*
Occurs annually, especially in spring. Bred in the south-east of the county in the 1960s for several years.

HEN HARRIER *(Circus cyaneus)*
Still unwarrantably persecuted. The male of a breeding pair was shot in a central moorland area in 1974. Breeding occurs in the west, where additional birds have been seen summering on tracts of country suitable for nesting. Wintering birds, usually singles, are reported in both hill and lowland areas.

MONTAGU'S HARRIER *(Circus pygargus)*
A somewhat unpredictable species which nests periodically, more especially in the north-east and latterly in East Yorkshire.

OSPREY *(Pandion haliaetus)*
A passage migrant, the Osprey occurs by reservoirs and rivers during the spring and autumn migration period, with records from Gouthwaite, Fairburn Ings, Wath Ings, Stocks Reservoir (Bowland) and the lake at Castle Howard. A pole with a cart-wheel on top may be seen on an island in Stocks Reservoir, where it was hoped to encourage Ospreys to nest.

HOBBY *(Falco subbuteo)*
Odds birds occur mainly in May and August-September. At the latter period they often obtain their food by attacking hirundines going to roost.

PEREGRINE FALCON *(Falco peregrinus)*
Possibly no more than one pair of these attractive falcons occur annually in Yorkshire. The Peregrine formerly nested on the Yorkshire coast. Wintering birds noted and the 1974 bird report of the Y.N.U. recorded an immature bird pursuing House Martins at Flamborough Head on September 1, an adult chasing gulls at Stocks Reservoir on November 17, and a third in pursuit of ducks and Herons at the same reservoir on December 14.

MERLIN *(Falco columbarius)*

A few breeding pairs occur in moorland situations on the Pennines, especially the eastern spurs, and on the north-east moors. Single birds reported from various parts in autumn and early winter, when birds leave moorland nesting areas.

KESTREL *(Falco tinnunculus)*

Relatively common and widespread. At nesting time has used the old nests of other species. Man-made sites include mill chimneys, electricity pylons, pit winding-gear and even Leeds Town Hall.

RED GROUSE *(Lagopus lagopus)*

The highest population of Red Grouse is associated with *Calluna* moorland, the best examples of which are on the eastern spurs of the Pennines, notably around Wharfedale and Nidderdale, and also the northern part of the north-east bloc. Several pairs breed on Tarn Moss, Malham Moor. On the high Pennines, a few Red Grouse frequent *Nardus* and *Eriophorum* moors. The best time to see Red Grouse is in early spring, when cock grouse, in particular, take up positions on roadside walls. A motorist on one of the many moorland roads may then pass within a few yards of the birds. Parent birds with broods of young also seen close to roads in July.

BLACK GROUSE *(Lyrurus tetrix)*

A local breeding species which appears to be increasing. Most common on *Nardus* ground and at young conifer forests in the west, especially Upper Teesdale, Tan Hill, Malham Moor and west of Ribblesdale. In Upper Wharfedale an observer at a *lek* in March, 1974, counted 150 males, an exceptional number.

RED-LEGGED PARTRIDGE *(Alectoris rufa)*

Occurs on the Wolds, in and around the Vale of Pickering, in the Knaresborough district and commonly in south-east Yorkshire.

PARTRIDGE *(Perdix perdix)*

Now well established again in the west after being somewhat scarce, but intensive agricultural practices and the use of chemicals reduced the population in the arable areas of the east. The Partridge is common in the Midgely/Bretton area, and here the national decline in the population was less evident.

COMMON PHEASANT *(Phasianus colchicus)*

Most common in the vicinity of large estates, where birds are hatched out in incubators and raised for sport. Escapees from the autumnal slaughter sometimes find sanctuary and nesting opportunities in areas newly planted with conifers.

73

WATER RAIL *(Rallus aquaticus)*
At some Yorkshire locations breeding of this reclusive species has been suspected but not proved. Possible nesting areas include: Fairburn Ings, Blacktoft Sands (Goole), Potteric Carr. With the autumnal die-back of vegetation, the Water Rail is more easily seen as at Bretton, Swillington and Mickletown Ings and Newmillerdam.

CORNCRAKE *(Crex crex)*
Once common and well distributed in summer in farming areas, the Corncrake has suffered a serious decline, largely because of changes in agricultural practice. A few birds are reported annually. A pair was reported from an allotment at Barnoldswick in 1974 but did not nest successfully because of interference.

MOORHEN *(Gallinula chloropus)*
A common breeding species not only on the larger lakes but also on small ponds and along watercourses. Nests usually at—or a little above—water level but tree-nesting is not uncommon, especially on the Huddersfield canal where bankside hawthorns are regularly used.

COOT *(Fulica atra)*
The many breeding haunts include Hornsea Mere (up to 200 pairs), Malham Tarn, Bretton and Newmillerdam. Flocks from late summer, with up to 1,000 birds gathering at Fairburn Ings and Hornsea Mere (over 3,000 at Hornsea in December, 1971) and several hundred at many other waters.

OYSTERCATCHER *(Haematopous ostralegus)*
Nesting pairs frequent lowland gravel pits and river shingle having spread inland from the west coast. Some Dales pairs nest at over 1,000 feet. An increasing number of birds choose to nest in fields adjacent to watercourses rather than on shingle. Few pairs nest on the Yorkshire coast but large offshore movements observed with assemblies on the estuaries of Tees and Humber. Birds visit the mussel beds north of White Nab, Scarborough.

LAPWING *(Vanellus vanellus)*
A distinctive breeding species on pasture and moorland up to around 1,500 feet on the Pennines. Also breeds on lowland farms and sewage works in the industrial areas of West Yorkshire though some authorities claim it is decreasing as a breeding species in lowland Britain. Post-breeding flocks may be of immense size, with assemblies of 1,000 to 2,000 birds recorded from the Ribble Valley of the far west, to the Lower Derwent floods of central Yorkshire, and the mudflats of the Humber estuary. An especially large assembly of Lapwings was an estimated 5,000-plus by the Derwent in late December 1974. About

1,200 birds were present at Walton Hall (Wakefield) in November 1972. Over-wintering of birds at Gouthwaite in mild winters.

RINGED PLOVER *(Charadrius hiaticula)*
Mainly a coastal nesting species whose numbers have decreased through increased human disturbance. Nesting pairs at Spurn declined from 70 (in 1914) to 36 (1936), 20 (1949), 10 (1974). A few pairs breed inland. Passage migration along and through the Pennines in spring and autumn.

LITTLE RINGED PLOVER *(Charadrius dubius)*
First reported as breeding in 1947, since when it has nested at a number of gravel pits and flash sites at fairly low elevation. Sites include Fairburn Ings, Farnham, the lower Aire Valley, and Seamer, near Scarborough. Probably over 40 pairs in Yorkshire in any one year.

GREY PLOVER *(Pluvialis squatarola)*
A winter visitor to the coast, the Grey Plover is especially associated with the Humber estuary. Occasional occurrences inland of small parties of birds during periods of migration, especially in May and from August to September. The striking black and silver breeding plumage is occasionally seen.

GOLDEN PLOVER *(Pluvialis apricaria)*
Nests at sites around the 1,500 feet contour line but breeders found at up to 2,000 feet on some fells in Craven and also at the southern end of the Pennines. Also breeds on high ground in the east, including Jugger Howe. Quite large wintering flocks on farmland in the Wolds and the Carrs, also Derwent Valley and the Settle and Clapham areas. Spring flocks of northern-type birds have been seen at Durkar, Kirkthorpe and in the Ribble Valley.

DOTTEREL *(Eudromias morinellus)*
"Trips" of Dotterel pass through Yorkshire on their way to northern breeding grounds. Few birds are seen in the eastern areas, where formerly there was a strong movement (notice the *Dotterel Inn,* near Reighton). Flocks wantonly reduced by marksmen. Recent sightings of Dotterel on Blubberhouses Moor, Rombald's Moor, Ingleborough and the ridges near Wensleydale.

TURNSTONE *(Arenaria interpres)*
Present on coast in winter months and up to May when birds are assuming breeding plumage. Return passage noted from July onwards with several hundred birds present in some coastal areas. Occasionally seen at inland areas in small numbers.

SNIPE *(Gallinago gallinago)*
Quite common as a nesting species from lowlands to marshy areas up to 1,300 feet; less common in the south-east. On high

ground in particular, nests may be found well into summer, by which time some birds are flocking in lowland areas. Autumn assemblies reported from various places, including Gouthwaite.

JACK SNIPE *(Lymnocryptes minimus)*
Frequently flushed from marshy areas in winter, but in small numbers compared with the Snipe, with which it frequently associates.

WOODCOCK *(Scolopax rusticola)*
A widely-spread breeding species, less so in the east. Occurs mainly in woodland in hill areas, but a pair nested in a garden at Summerbridge (Nidderdale) in 1972. Springtime "roding" by cock birds can establish the presence of nesting Woodcock. One bird regularly flies across the lawn at Malham Tarn House. Large numbers of continental Woodcock may arrive on the east coast in late autumn.

CURLEW *(Numenius arquata)*
Breeding pairs most common on hill land and the upper and middle reaches of the Dales from about 600 to 1,100 feet, but in recent decades has nested at lower elevations and become wide-spread. Assemblies of Pennine birds seen in mid-June, first on moderately high ground and then in the dales. About 2,000 birds have been seen in the Ribble Valley near Rathmell in late August and other well-known assembly areas at Malham and Stocks. Over-wintering by a small flock of Curlew at Gouthwaite Reservoir.

WHIMBREL *(Numenius phaeopus)*
Many records of birds on coastal passage, especially in May and July/September. Regular sightings of a few Whimbrel at inland areas.

BLACK-TAILED GODWIT *(Limosa limosa)*
A passage migrant in small numbers in spring and autumn, this godwit is likely to occur in any part of Yorkshire where standing water and rough pastures form an attraction. Frequent spring birds in breeding plumage give hope that this attractive species may again become established as one of our nesting birds.

BAR-TAILED GODWIT *(Limosa lapponica)*
This passage migrant is observed more often at the coast than is the Black-tailed Godwit, with over 100 birds at times at Spurn. More inland occurrences than usual in 1974 when 126 were at Fairburn on 20 April.

GREEN SANDPIPER *(Tringa ochropus)*
Mainly a passage migrant in spring and autumn and more particularly inland. Increasing tendency for birds to over-winter in Yorkshire.

WOOD SANDPIPER *(Tringa glareola)*
Small numbers often seen inland in May and again in early autumn.

COMMON SANDPIPER *(Tringa hypoleucos)*
Fairly common as a breeding species in the central and western parts of Yorkshire. Nesting occurs beside rivers and streams and also by reservoirs and tarns. Migration is strong from about mid-April (though some birds arrive earlier) and most breeding areas have been vacated by mid-September. Odd birds may remain in Yorkshire throughout October.

REDSHANK *(Tringa totanus)*
Was at one time mainly restricted to coastal marshes, but has now established itself in hill country, where it arrives to breed in March. The Redshank is especially common on the Pennines. Wintering groups in moist and temperate parts of Yorkshire, especially about the mouth of the Humber where 1,700 were observed in November 1971 and Tees (1,200 in September that year). Small numbers reported from various places including Swillington Ings and Wintersett Reservoir.

SPOTTED REDSHANK *(Tringa erythropus)*
Passage birds seen in May are not infrequently in their striking full breeding plumage. Autumn birds are often most readily picked out from the Common Redshanks by their distinctive call.

GREENSHANK *(Tringa nebularia)*
Passage migrant in spring and autumn both in coastal and inland areas where birds are increasingly reported in the winter months. Greenshank moving inland linger at reservoirs and marshland. Regular sightings in the Ribble Valley, on Dewsbury Moor, Wath Ings, Swillington and Fairburn among others.

KNOT *(Calidris canutus)*
Passage migrant. Large flocks on the coast. The number at Spurn in February and October can reach 2,000. A few birds use inland routes at migration time.

PURPLE SANDPIPER *(Calidris maritima)*
In order to be sure of seeing this winter visitor it is necessary to visit rocky areas such as Filey Brigg or Robin Hood's Bay.

LITTLE STINT *(Calidris minuta)*
A frequent autumn passage bird, less frequent in spring. Both coastal and more particularly inland sightings.

TEMMINCK'S STINT *(Calidris temminckii)*
Less frequently seen on migration than Little Stint, but a pair bred in central Yorkshire in 1951.

DUNLIN *(Calidris alpina)*

Also known as plover's page. Sparsely distributed as a nesting species on the Pennines, frequenting moist ground at over 1,500 feet. Prefers areas where there is some standing water—tarns on the Craven Pennines, reservoirs further south. Dunlin are seen in quite large numbers at the coast when migrating, and at peak times there can be 2,000 at Spurn Point. Wintering groups at Jackson's Bay and Cornelian Bay, Scarborough; also Filey Brigg. Cliff-top roosting has been reported. In winter small numbers may frequent wet arable fields in lowland areas of east Yorkshire.

CURLEW SANDPIPER *(Calidris testacea)*

Passage migrant seen in good numbers in some autumns and often associated with the best movements of Little Stints.

SANDERLING *(Calidris alba)*

As many as 300 birds may be seen at some coastal areas in winter. Inland, the Sanderling occurs only in small numbers and normally only at migration times, especially May and September/October.

RUFF *(Philomachus pugnax)*

A frequently-recorded passage migrant in April/May and July/September. The May-time birds often in breeding plumage. There is every hope that Ruff will resume breeding in the county as they have done elsewhere in Britain.

GREAT SKUA *(Stercorarius skua)*

Passage migrant off the coast. A few birds are reported in spring, rather more during autumn migration. Inland occasionally. One at Fairburn took a Coot as prey.

POMARINE SKUA *(Stercorarius pomarinus)*

Passage migrant off the coast. Most frequent records from Tees-mouth.

ARCTIC SKUA *(Stercorarius parasiticus)*

As a passage migrant, Arctic Skua is the member of this family most commonly seen by coastal watchers. In autumn, numbers can exceed 400 a day. Most birds when moving to wintering grounds stay well away from the coast unless driven inshore by strong winds. The Arctic Skua is also attracted by large numbers of Kittiwakes and terns. Then both the birds of the year and adults with the longer central tail feathers can be seen chasing these two species to induce them to yield their latest catch.

GREAT BLACK-BACKED GULL *(Larus marinus)*

Several pairs of Great Black-backed Gulls nest at a large colony of Lessers on the Bowland Fells. Elsewhere, predominantly a winter visitor which may be seen at refuse tips. Winter roosts include reservoirs: Ardsley, Wintersett, Blackmoorfoot, Gouthwaite, Barden, Washburndale, also Swillington Ings, Fairburn

78

Ings and some other waters on the eastern side of the Pennines. A maximum of 700 birds was seen at Ardsley in the winter of 1972. The Great Black-backed Gull is one of the scavengers in Dales lambing fields in spring. Several hundred seen on autumn passage at the coast, especially in the Tees and Humber estuaries.

LESSER BLACK-BACKED GULL *(Larus fuscus)*

Breeding species. Present at a large gullery on the Bowland fells and Stainmore; reported to have nested at a moorland site in Craven. Attempts have been made by gamekeepers to eliminate the moorland colonies but the habit of inland nesting appears to spread. Elsewhere, a non-breeding summer visitor. Traditionally, this species migrated to the Iberian peninsula and northwest Africa, but the presence of a continual supply of food at tips has encouraged many birds to remain through the winter. Assemblies at winter roosts on Pennine tarns and reservoirs, including Gouthwaite.

HERRING GULL *(Larus argentatus)*

Well represented at a large gullery on the Bowland fells. Also nests on rooftops at Whitby and Scarborough—there were about 500 nesting pairs in 1976—and on any suitable cliffs along the coast. Winter roosting at inland reservoirs. The number at Ardsley in 1972 peaked at about 5,000 on November 25, with few birds present on the following night, creating speculation that the species varies its roosting places more than do other large gulls.

COMMON GULL *(Larus canus)*

A pair is reported to have nested by a moorland tarn in Wharfedale, but most Common Gulls seen in Yorkshire in winter are from northern breeding grounds. Roosting on reservoirs and other large stretches of water, with an estimated 1,000 at Ardsley in December 1972. About 6,000 birds were present at Eccup Reservoir in late September, 1974. Common Gulls frequent playing fields and other areas of mown grass including Harrogate Stray.

GLAUCOUS GULL *(Larus hyperboreus)* and
ICELAND GULL *(Larus glaucoides)*

Two species which occur in winter months and may be found occasionally among flocks of larger gulls at inland rubbish tips, and also on the coast, notably at Scarborough Harbour or Filey.

MEDITERRANEAN GULL *(Larus melanocephalus)*

Increasingly reported, mainly from the coast, with birds now fairly regular at Scarborough in winter.

LITTLE GULL *(Larus minutus)*

Increasingly reported both on the coast and inland—the latter especially after easterly winds during migration periods.

BLACK-HEADED GULL *(Larus ridibundus)*

Commonest and most widespread of the nesting gulls, with a large breeding colony on Thorne Moor and smaller colonies by many Pennine hill tarns, at Skipwith Common, Knostrop, Fairburn, etc. Considerable gullery on island in Stocks Reservoir. Winter roosts can be of immense size, with maxima of 10,000 noted at Fairburn Ings and 13,500 at Ardsley Reservoir. Other waters to watch: Wintersett, Eccup, Blackmoorfoot Reservoirs, Malham Tarn, Peasholm (Scarborough). Ringing has shown that many of the birds that breed in Yorkshire move south and west (including Eire) while our winter flocks include birds from the Baltic countries.

KITTIWAKE *(Rissa tridactyla)*

Large colonies on the coast, with estimated 53,000 pairs at Bempton Cliffs (1975). A further large concentration of nests on Flamborough Head. Kittiwakes began to colonise Scarborough Castle hill during the 1939-45 war; there are now an estimated 1,700 pairs, with a small colony established just north of Long Nab. A few migrating birds reported from inland waters March/June. Large numbers of Kittiwakes seen off the coast in all months.

BLACK TERN *(Chlidonias niger)*

At times when strong easterlies blow, a few birds may be seen on spring and autumn passage at inland locations. Sightings include Stocks Reservoir (in the far west) and Hornsea Mere (near the coast), with many waters in between. Spurn provides most of the coastal records.

COMMON/ARCTIC TERN *(Sterna hirundo/paradisaea)*

A regular migrant in large numbers on the coast. Congregates at Spurn in late July and early August and feeds off-shore. Reported from many inland locations, with evidence of cross-country movement especially in May.

LITTLE TERN *(Sterna albifrons)*

Formerly nested in strength at Spurn, but now seen only in small numbers anywhere on the coast. A few records of inland passage birds.

SANDWICH TERN *(Sterna sandvicensis)*

Birds pass northwards along the coast in April/May for their breeding grounds. Autumn passage extends mainly from late July to September, with up to 4,000 birds seen in southward flight on a single day in early September at that prime point of observation, Spurn Point. A few inland sightings.

RAZORBILL *(Alca torda)*

Nests on the chalk cliffs from Speeton to Flamborough. A census on the Bempton stretch in early July 1975 revealed 3,395.

LITTLE AUK *(Alle alle)*

Seen off the Yorkshire coast in autumn and winter, usually after northerly gales when single birds often join incoming flocks of immigrant Starlings. Storm-driven birds have been found exhausted inland.

GUILLEMOT *(Uria aalge)*

Considerable numbers nest on the cliffs between Speeton and Flamborough with nesting on cliffs north of Filey suspected. Census at Bempton in 1975 showed 12,879; small percentage of the bridled form. Oiled birds all too frequently seen along the coast.

PUFFIN *(Fratercula arctica)*

Breeding species. Estimated 2,500 on Bempton and Flamborough cliffs. Yorkshire Puffins tend to use holes or crannies between rocks as nesting places and do not burrow into grassy slopes at the cliff top.

STOCK DOVE *(Columba oenas)*

Relatively common in the west, nesting in holes in trees, and cliff and quarry faces. The presence of many farm buildings, especially those that are derelict, gives it some handy nesting sites on the Pennines. Breeds on Malham Cove. In eastern lowland areas, trees more exclusively used. Some quite large flocks —100 birds—have been reported in autumn.

ROCK DOVE *(Columba livia)*

The purity of birds breeding in holes and caves at Flamborough Head is in doubt. There has almost certainly been cross-breeding with domestic strains of pigeon.

WOODPIGEON *(Columba palumbus)*

Abundant. Numbers are increasing because of nesting and roosting opportunities provided by new conifer forests. In the west, dependent largely on the seeds of grasses and fruit of trees—i.e. beech mast—for food; in the east, late summer and autumn provide an abundance of grain. Wintering flocks can be of large size; an especially large group near Knaresborough in December, 1974, had an estimated 10,000 birds.

TURTLE DOVE *(Streptopelia turtur)*

A summer visitor from May/September. Most numerous in the east and south of the county. Its haunts include Midgley, Bretton, Cawthorne and many other areas.

COLLARED DOVE *(Streptopelia decaocto)*

Though relatively new, the Collared Dove is spreading rapidly. Flocks of around 200 birds noted in autumn. Like Turtle Dove, it is absent from the high Pennine areas.

CUCKOO *(Cuculus canorus)*

A fairly widespread visitor for breeding—though less common than it was—the Cuckoo parasitises smaller birds, the Meadow Pipit being a common host to its eggs in hill areas. Main influx of Cuckoos about April 20, and birds have been known to linger in Yorkshire until September.

BARN OWL *(Tyto alba)*

Not common, but population appears steady after a considerable decline over the past 50 years. Factors leading to its reduced numbers include the widespread use of rodent poisons. Successful breeding is regular adjacent to industrial areas. Most frequent observations result from birds being seen in car headlights. Many road casualties.

LITTLE OWL *(Athene noctua)*

Introduced to Walton Park by Charles Waterton in 1842. Now found as a nesting species in all parts of Yorkshire. May be seen in daylight perched on walls or buildings.

TAWNY OWL *(Strix aluco)*

Commonest of the Yorkshire owl species, being equally at home in deciduous and coniferous woods, in the country, and in suburban areas with large gardens. A common casualty on road and rail.

LONG-EARED OWL *(Asio otus)*

Denizen of old pinewoods, this species is now benefiting from maturing stands in the new conifer forests, though it is less common than it was, possibly because of competition from an increased population of Tawny Owls. Hawthorn thickets also favoured and old nests of others species used. Most pairs of Long-eared Owls occur in the southern part of Yorkshire, but breeding in the Bowland district has also been proved. Communal roosts a feature in some areas.

SHORT-EARED OWL *(Asio flammeus)*

A ground-nesting owl, frequenting marginal ground in the west, where the number of pairs can be locally high in "vole years". Areas of new planting with small conifers are especially attractive. The population in the upper Hodder Valley, in the west, peaked at seven pairs but is now generally one or two. Also reported from lowland areas, including east Yorkshire. Spurn has an immigration of continental birds in autumn. A bird ringed as a nestling in Gisburn Forest was found in Kent during the following winter.

NIGHTJAR *(Caprimulgus europaeus)*

Though generally less common than formerly, its haunts include moorland near Ripon, Washburn Valley, upper Wharfedale, Cawthorne, Newmillerdam and Woolley; Thorne and Hatfield

Moor in the south and east; Skipwith Common near York; Birch Hall and Silpho near Scarborough.

SWIFT *(Apus apus)*

Nests under the roofs of buildings. Conspicuous by its screaming call at many towns and villages in Yorkshire; birds are seen hawking for insect life above the high hills of the west. Large concentration of birds over lowland waters such as Fairburn when there is a hatch of insects.

KINGFISHER *(Atthis alcedo)*

Wide though thin distribution in Yorkshire. Recovery of this species from the 1962-63 winter was gradual. Nowhere very common, but reasonable numbers in the Craven district, where rivers and streams run clear and with deep pools.

GREEN WOODPECKER *(Picus viridis)*

Occurs in the north and west, where it prefers lightly wooded situations, such as fellside woods in the dales, but commonest in lower areas of mature woodland or park-like conditions, including north of Pickering Vale and to the north and west of Scarborough. Breeds in suitable wooded areas adjacent to some west Yorkshire towns and cities. The Green Woodpecker appears to have become more common than the Great Spotted in some areas; in others it has not reappeared at haunts where it became absent during the hard winter of 1962/3. Commonly known as the Yaffle, from its call.

GREAT SPOTTED WOODPECKER *(Dendrocopos major)*

Thought to have declined numerically. Fairly common in some southern and western areas of broad-leafed woodland, also at the southern edge of the North York Moors.

LESSER SPOTTED WOODPECKER *(Dendrocopos minor)*

A species which is often overlooked. Occurs where the dales extend eastwards to the heart of the county, also in Bowland and south Yorkshire.

SKYLARK *(Alauda arvensis)*

Well distributed as a nesting species from the coast to high and marginal· ground, to which it returns usually in March. Moderately large flocks seen in various places in autumn and winter. In autumn a conspicuous southward passage of Skylarks occurs at the Yorkshire coast, further winter movements being stimulated by the onset of hard weather.

SHORE LARK *(Eremophila alpestris)*

A winter visitor to coastal areas in small numbers. The Tees estuary, Spurn and Filey are the favoured spots.

SWALLOW *(Hirundo rustica)*

Nests mainly in farm buildings in rural areas. Pairs may be

found nesting at high elevations—frequently at 1,000 feet above sea level on the Craven Pennines. Sites near sea level include former gun emplacements at Spurn. Large autumnal roosts notably at Fairburn Ings, with up to 100,000 birds reported in September. Ringing has shown that our birds winter in South Africa. The first birds arrive in April and most have left by the end of October.

HOUSE MARTIN *(Delichon urbica)*
Breeding range largely dependent on the availability of buildings (with nesting at over 1,000 feet on stations of the Settle-Carlisle railway); also frequents cliff sites in places, including Kilnsey Crag (Wharfedale) and Flamborough. House Martins are generally distributed by the end of May and birds may frequently be seen as late as October or early November.

SAND MARTIN *(Riparia riparia)*
Possibly less common than it was. Colonies in sandy banks of rivers, also sandpits away from water, even temporary heaps of fine material at quarries in the dales. Small nesting colony in western bank of Malham Tarn, and another at Sandal (Wakefield) brickworks. Post-nesting roost at Fairburn Ings, with estimated 20,000 birds in early September. Present from end of March to September/October.

RAVEN *(Corvus corax)*
A scarce nesting species virtually confined to the fells in the north-west. The Raven was, until about 1860, a breeding species on the chalk cliffs of the Yorkshire coast. Wanderers from the northern Pennines—and especially the young of the year—may be seen in winter in the western dales country.

CARRION CROW *(Corvus corone)*
Now very common in some hill districts. Territorial pressure in high valley near Settle led to attempted nesting on walltops in 1975 and 1976. Semi-albino crows reported in the west. Winter roost of up to 100 birds in various districts. The HOODED CROW occurs in winter months, mainly at the coast but occasionally inland also.

ROOK *(Corvus frugilegus)*
Locally common on low ground in good farming country, with a few high elevation rookeries. The Rook is seen feeding on high grassland areas in the west during the spring and summer, being reported at up to 1,700 feet. Impressive flightlines to winter roosts; pre-roost assemblies blacken the ground nearby.

JACKDAW *(Corvus monedula)*
Breeding sites in quarries up to about 1,300 feet and holes in crags; nests on cliffs of Flamborough and Bempton and also holes in trees and chimney stacks. Small colonies in some church

towers. Large winter flocks commute to roost. Semi-albino Jackdaw reported from Settle district 1975 and 1976.

MAGPIE *(Pica pica)*

Well established and becoming increasingly common in many districts, not only near farms and villages but the industrial areas of the west, especially any leafy suburbs. Groups in excess of 20 frequently reported in autumn and winter. Up to 40 birds roosted in woodland near Leeds at the year end, 1974. Other roosts have been recorded with 100 (Sowood), and 85 (Ogden Reservoir).

JAY *(Garrulus glandarius)*

Well established in woodland at fairly low elevation to the east of the Pennines, in the suburbs of several towns and cities and also in the Bowland area, with recent emissaries to woodland at the foothills of Ingleborough. Well represented in the Harrogate/Ripon area.

GREAT TIT *(Parus major)*

Moderately common in lowland gardens and woods, but has also been found breeding at over 1,000 feet on the Pennines, frequenting old deciduous woodland there. The tits have benefited greatly by the increase in the habit of people feeding birds in the winter and providing nest boxes.

BLUE TIT *(Parus caeruleus)*

Well distributed in gardens and deciduous woodland, where it may become temporarily more numerous during the winter as groups of Blue Tits and other tit species—Long-tailed, Great, Coal—move in small mixed flocks.

COAL TIT *(Parus ater)*

Pre-eminently of coniferous woodland and the principal user of nesting boxes placed in such areas.

MARSH TIT *(Parus palustris)*

Prefers mature woodland. Difficult to distinguish in the field from the Willow Tit. Song and call only certain points of identification from harsh grating of Willow Tit.

WILLOW TIT *(Parus montanus)*

Common in scrubby woodland of old willow, birch, alder and elder trees, the presence of which it needs at nesting time as it excavates its own nesting hole.

LONG-TAILED TIT *(Aegithalos caudatus)*

Population has risen considerably as a consequence of a series of mild winters. Prolonged snow and ice severely reduce numbers of this frail-looking bird. Wintering flocks of 30/40 birds often reported.

NUTHATCH *(Sitta europaea)*

Widely distributed but curiously local with few in the north and west. Mature broad-leaved timber is a prerequisite, but even where this exists the bird is not always present. Good haunts include: Duncombe Park (Helmsley), Bretton Park, Studley Royal and Grantley. The Nuthatch is seen in wooded areas of Wharfedale to just above Grassington.

TREECREEPER *(Certhia familiaris)*

A resident breeder in woodlands, the Treecreeper appears most commonly in old oak woods where loose bark on dead trees provides nesting sites. Will also nest in tree cavities and behind thick stems of ivy. Associates with tit flocks in autumn and winter.

WREN *(Troglodytes troglodytes)*

Is found from near sea level to the highest crags where, in mid-winter, it may be the only bird to be seen and heard.

DIPPER *(Cinclus cinclus)*

Typical of the swift, clear streams of the Pennine fells and dales, but also moderately common in the north-east, especially the Howardian Hills. The Dipper is sedentary; birds rarely stray more than a mile or so from the place where they were hatched. Nests under banks and bridges, with trees used as song-posts, but equally at home on moorland streams.

BEARDED TIT *(Panurus biarmicus)*

Nesting for some 12/15 years at Blacktoft Sands, near Goole, in which area quite large numbers are now seen. With general increase over the country as a whole, birds of this species now appear at other areas during periods of dispersal — e.g., Minsmere-ringed birds at Wintersett and Nostell in the autumn of 1973.

MISTLE THRUSH *(Turdus viscivorus)*

Also known as Stormcock. Can be common in many areas, with nesting frequent close to human habitations. Also quite common in some wooded hill districts of the east.

FIELDFARE *(Turdus pilaris)*

Large autumnal arrivals of continental Fieldfares at the Yorkshire coast. This visitor for the winter is frequently seen in open country and gills with berried trees from October. Sightings for August are on record, and flocks may still be seen in April, more unusually in May. By spring it is largely a ground feeder.

SONG THRUSH *(Turdus philomelos)*

A widely distributed nester and in some areas, where the shrub layer is thin, has been found nesting on the ground (reported from Malham Tarn, North Craven and Bowland), and may also nest on walls. A familiar bird in the garden. Influx of continental birds in autumn when our own nesters tend to move south and west.

REDWING *(Turdus iliacus)*
Winter visitor, less numerous than the Fieldfare. First big influx usually early October, with Spurn as a good place to look for newly arrived continental birds. Lingers in Yorkshire until April. Roosts of up to 500 Redwings are on record. A bird caught and ringed at Spurn was recovered, in the following year, from Italy.

RING OUZEL *(Turdus torquatus)*
In general terms, the breeding areas of the lowland Blackbird and hill-going Ring Ouzel meet at about 1,000 feet; in fact a considerable overlap occurs, and in Upper Teesdale the Blackbird is a common breeder above 1,000 feet. The Ring Ouzel is commoner on the western edges of the Pennines than areas to the east. Nesting on the southern Pennines is rarely below 800 feet. The species is occasionally seen in rocky gills on the north-east moors. First arrivals are noticed in March; there is some flocking by the end of July, and the nesting areas are usually clear of birds by the third week in September. Over-wintering of a few birds in western Yorkshire during mild periods is suspected.

BLACKBIRD *(Turdus merula)*
The Blackbird is one of the most familiar breeding birds in Yorkshire, frequenting a wide range of habitats. It is also a winter visitor with large numbers arriving on the east coast in late October and early November. An exceptionally large roost, at a plantation in mid-Wharfedale, in late October 1974, held about 3,000 birds.

WHEATEAR *(Oenanthe oenanthe)*
One of the first of the migrant bird arrivals, being seen in late March. Quite common on the Pennines where rock outcrops, drystone walls and old rabbit burrows offer nesting possibilities. Main departure complete by mid-October. Seen in many lowland areas during migration.

STONECHAT *(Saxicola torquata)*
Only casual as a breeding species. Among its Yorkshire haunts are Jugger Howe, Scarborough, and it has nested near Leeds. Occurs regularly in the autumn and winter months, even though it is widely and thinly scattered.

WHINCHAT *(Saxicola rubetra)*
Locally common, the Whinchat nests on rough ground in lowland areas and also on moor edges and in new plantations. First arrivals noted in April. The species is present in numbers in early May, and until September/October.

REDSTART *(Phoenicurus phoenicurus)*

Nests in the older deciduous woodland of the dales, also quite often in drystone walls. Almost invariably the first bird to be heard calling—usually half an hour before first light—during May and June. Less common in lowland, eastern part of the county.

BLACK REDSTART *(Phoenicurus ochrurus)*

Several records of breeding in recent years. Most often seen as a migrant on the coast in later March-April and September to October.

ROBIN *(Erithacus rubecula)*

This bird is so commonly known that many people do not appreciate that large numbers of continental birds arrive on the east coast in autumn. In the first week of October 1951, over 600 Robins were ringed at Spurn with subsequent evidence of them moving on to France, Italy, Minorca, etc.

NIGHTINGALE *(Luscinia megarhynchos)*

Uncommon. Breeding has occurred in south Yorkshire. Night singers, often reported, are usually found to be Sedge Warblers.

GRASSHOPPER WARBLER *(Locustella naevia)*

The total nesting population is relatively small, but pairs are well distributed, though less commonly in the dales. The Grasshopper Warbler is most numerous in the south and east of the county. Has been found nesting in areas of young coniferous plantations.

REED WARBLER *(Acrocephalus scirpaceus)*

Yorkshire is the northern limit of the range on the eastern side of the Pennines. Beds of phragmites form the commonest habitat. Main colonies are at Hornsea Mere, Fairburn and Swillington Ings, Thorne Moors, Blacktoft Sands (200 pairs at the latter place in 1974).

SEDGE WARBLER *(Acrocephalus schoenobaenus)*

Thinly distributed but more widespread than the Reed Warbler. Generally in low-lying and moist habitats.

BLACKCAP *(Sylvia atricapilla)*

Generally though thinly distributed. Nests in the shrub layer of woodland, but needs trees for feeding and as song-posts. Overwintering recorded.

GARDEN WARBLER *(Sylvia borin)*

Thinly but widely distributed. Like the Blackcap, it utilises trees for feeding and singing but nests within a few feet of the ground.

WHITETHROAT *(Sylvia communis)*

Summer visitor from mid-April to mid-September, with odd birds remaining in October. Still scarce and sporadic after quite drastic fall in the population in 1960. Fond of nesting in railway cuttings and roadside hedgerows where its presence is betrayed by its song-flights.

LESSER WHITETHROAT *(Sylvia curruca)*
Often overlooked by those who do not recognise its song. Breeds sparingly in many areas—more commonly in eastern lowlands of the county. Passage birds occur after east winds in May and in autumn.

WILLOW WARBLER *(Phylloscopus trochilus)*
The commonest of the warblers, breeding up to an elevation of 1,000 feet in high-level woodland in the Pennines and at even higher levels in young coniferous areas where sufficient open space is available for its nest on the ground. Can be numerous during periods of migration, and then visits suburban gardens in late summer where it can be seen taking aphids from rose bushes.

CHIFFCHAFF *(Phylloscopus collybita)*
One of the first spring migrants. Generally distributed, with main influx of birds usually in the first week of April, some 7 or 10 days before the arrival of the Willow Warbler. Occasional winter records.

WOOD WARBLER *(Phylloscopus sibilatrix)*
The strongholds of this summer visitor are in the north and west but several pairs do frequent Forge Valley near Scarborough. Sloping ground and the presence of beech trees seem to be favoured; the nest is on the ground.

GOLDCREST *(Regulus regulus)*
Quite high density of nesting pairs in new coniferous areas. Autumn immigration along east coast, especially in October. In the Holderness area it is known as the "Woodcock Pilot" because it was believed that so small a bird could not make the crossing of the sea without obtaining a lift from the larger birds.

FIRECREST *(Regulus ignicapillus)*
An uncommon migrant which frequents bracken and scrub near the coast, though it has been observed as far inland as the Bowland area.

SPOTTED FLYCATCHER *(Muscicapa striata)*
Widely but thinly distributed from upper dales to coast, especially in the vicinity of woods and watercourses, but possibly less common than it was.

PIED FLYCATCHER *(Ficedula hypoleuca)*
Nests in some old woods in the western dales, including those near Bolton Abbey and Ripon. Of late years, has been seen in urban areas, and it breeds successfully each year in the grounds

of a chemical works near Huddersfield. Readily takes to nest boxes.

DUNNOCK or HEDGE SPARROW *(Prunella modularis)*
Common and widespread resident bird, in suburban gardens as well as remote areas where sufficient cover occurs.

MEADOW PIPIT *(Anthus pratensis)*
Possibly the commonest of the hill birds, host of the Cuckoo and prey of Merlin. Although usually absent from the fells from October to February, it has been known to winter on the southern Pennines as well as the more customary lowland areas. Spring and autumn passage observed at Spurn and elsewhere, in March/April and September/October.

TREE PIPIT *(Anthus trivialis)*
A summer visitor frequenting open woodland, and heaths where there are scattered trees for perching, and from which it makes distinctive song-flights. A favourite habitat is a bracken slope with birch. In some areas, including South Yorkshire, Tree Pipit nests are favoured by Cuckoos.

ROCK PIPIT *(Anthus spinoletta)*
Breeds on rocky parts of the Yorkshire coast, in the vicinity of Boulby, Scarborough and Flamborough. Feeds mostly on the shore, but is occasionally reported inland. Spring passage of Scandinavian Rock Pipit detected on the coast.

PIED WAGTAIL *(Motacilla alba)*
A resident species, but a summer visitor to hill areas. On the Pennines and in the dales, drystone walls are frequently chosen as nesting places. Large roosts of Pied Wagtails in late summer have been reported from lowland areas east of the Pennines and winter roosts include Ferrybridge Power Station. White Wagtails which nests in more northerly regions, are often identified on passage in April and early May.

GREY WAGTAIL *(Motacilla cinerea)*
A visitor for breeding, the Grey Wagtail is a bird of clear hill streams, The species is most common in the western dales, but these areas are deserted in winter when it moves to lower ground.

YELLOW WAGTAIL *(Motacilla flava)*
This summer visitor is widely spread throughout Yorkshire in the breeding season, nesting commonly in the north and west, in the dales and also on hill pastures up to about 1,500 feet, and throughout many lowland parts of the county, but uncommon as a nester in east Yorkshire. Large roosts form in reed beds in early autumn prior to the birds' departure. Breeds regularly in some areas near the outskirts of industrial towns in the south west.

WAXWING *(Bombycilla garrulus)*

This winter visitor varies in numbers. Spreading inland from the east coast, it is attracted by berries annually to many places including gardens in the far west. Roadside hawthorn and sorbus trees often present opportunities to see the bird at close quarters.

GREAT GREY SHRIKE *(Lanius excubitor)*

Arrival of birds on east coast mainly in October, and then birds (usually singly) scattered over a wide area during winter, leaving for northern breeding grounds in April.

RED-BACKED SHRIKE *(Lanius collurio)*

A spring and autumn passage migrant in small numbers, usually seen on the coast.

STARLING *(Sturnus vulgaris)*

Well-distributed, the Starling is everywhere a familiar bird. Large roosts of juveniles in late summer; winter roosts include plantations where well over 100,000 birds may assemble and also on buildings in some large towns—e.g. Bradford and Huddersfield. About 5,000 roosting birds have been seen at Peasholm, Scarborough.

HAWFINCH *(Coccothraustes coccothraustes)*

A widely spread but local and uncommon species, being reported from Garrowby, Rievaulx, Bolton Abbey, Studley Park. Pairs seen in other areas, but breeding not always confirmed. A species which is easily overlooked.

GREENFINCH *(Carduelis chloris)*

Has become a quite common resident nesting species. Conspicuous autumn passage at Spurn, where seeds of sea-rocket form a favourite food. Inland roosts in winter of over 500 birds.

GOLDFINCH *(Carduelis carduelis)*

This resident nesting species is now fairly common and widespread. Quite large flocks often reported outside the nesting season.

SISKIN *(Carduelis spinus)*

Has nested from time to time in the coniferous plantations of the west, and the North York Moors forest-land, also near Harrogate and Sheffield, but mainly regarded as a winter visitor. Flocks, often in company of Redpolls, encountered in waterside areas, and especially where there are alders. A new trait is visiting peanut-feeders on bird tables.

LINNET *(Carduelis cannabina)*

Widespread hedgerow nesting species; on the hills, often in gorse. The Linnet is a garden bird in some West Yorkshire towns. Wintering flocks may be seen in lowland areas often in association with finches.

TWITE *(Acanthis flavirostris)*

Nesting species which has increased its numbers and range. Associated in the main with the high moorland of south-west Yorkshire, below the Aire Gap. Breeds mainly at 1,000 feet contour, usually in clumps of heather, but tends to feed in pastures and meadows. Partial migrant in winter when birds are mainly on the coast or estuaries.

REDPOLL *(Acanthis flammea)*

Common nesting species which has greatly increased in recent years. Is to be found in suburban areas as well as in coniferous plantations and deciduous woodland. Silver birch an attractive species. Outside the nesting season, can be seen in moderately large flocks. Wintering birds may have the company of a few Siskins or Mealy or Arctic Redpolls from further north.

BULLFINCH *(Pyrrhula pyrrhula)*

This resident breeder is widespread, especially among thickets, conifer plantations and gorse commons. Increasingly seen in suburban gardens.

CROSSBILL *(Loxia curvirostra)*

This species is benefiting from increased afforestation with conifers, and has bred on a number of occasions in various parts of the county. Still regarded mainly as an immigrant (from later summer onwards) often in large numbers when there is a population explosion in Scandinavian and north-east breeding areas.

CHAFFINCH *(Fringilla coelebs)*

Common and well distributed nesting species though less common than formerly in many lowland areas. Has been found nesting up to the limit of the tree line on the high Pennines. Flocks of c. 200 birds have been reported in winter.

BRAMBLING *(Fringilla montifringilla)*

As a winter visitor arriving in October, the Brambling is often associated with other finches. Congregations of up to 2,000 Bramblings have been noted in Yorkshire, beech-mast providing an attraction. Winter roosts, each with a few hundred birds.

CORN BUNTING *(Emberiza calandra)*

Nesting species, mainly in the lowland areas of eastern Yorkshire. Roadside song-perches on bushes, telephone wires, etc., make it a conspicuous even if not very colourful species. Winter roosts included one with 220 birds at Hornsea Mere in January 1974.

YELLOWHAMMER *(Emberiza citrinella)*

Also known as scribble-lark from markings on eggs. Nests in the lower dales and across the arable lowland areas to the coast.

REED BUNTING *(Emberiza schoeniclus)*
Widely-spread nesting species especially around flashes in the southern part of Yorkshire, as at Mickletown and Swillington Ings, Thorne Moors, etc. Nesting sites include canal-side vegetation and sewage works. The Reed Bunting is also found in the lower and middle dales.

LAPLAND BUNTING *(Calcarius lapponicus)*
The Lapland Bunting is a winter visitor mainly to coastal areas, with most occurrences between September and December.

SNOW BUNTING *(Plectrophenas nivalis)*
A winter visitor, the Snow Bunting can be seen from October until March. In the Pennines is found on high ground, often at over 1,500 feet. Also occurs on the North York Moors but most often seen at the coast, and especially the estuaries.

TREE SPARROW *(Passer montanus)*
Distinguished by its chestnut cap and dark spot on the cheek, the Tree Sparrow is a common though local breeder. Most frequently met with in lowland eastern half of the county, especially where old hedgerow trees provide nesting holes. Passage pronounced at Spurn in September and October. Large flocks in winter, e.g. 200 at Esholt, Hatfield, Blackmoorfoot, Wroot, Melton and Otley—all in 1971.

Selected Bibliography

Chislett, R. (1952) *Yorkshire Birds,* A. Brown & Sons, Hull.

Coward, T. A. (1950) *The Birds of the British Isles and their Eggs,* Warne.

Dickens, R. F. and Pickup, J. D. (1973) *Fairburn and its Nature Reserve,* Dalesman.

Geroudet, P. (1965) *Water Birds with Webbed Feet,* Blandford.

Heinzel, H., Fitter, R., and Parslow, J. (1972) *The Birds of Britain,* Collins.

Mitchell, W. R. and Robson, R. W. (1973) *Pennine Birds,* Dalesman.

Nelson, T. H. and Clarke, W. E. (1907), *The Birds of Yorkshire* A. Brown & Sons, Hull.

Parslow, J. (1973) *Breeding Birds of Britain and Ireland,* Poyser.

Peterson, R., Mountfort, G., and Hollom, P. A. D. (1966) *A Field Guide to the Birds of Britain and Europe,* Collins.

Sharrock, J. T. R. (1976) *The Atlas of Breeding Birds in Britain and Ireland,* British Trust for Ornithology.

Vaughan, R. (1974) *Birds of the Yorkshire Coast,* Hendon.

Waterton, C. (1837) *Essays in Natural History,* Warne.

Witherby, H. F. et al (1938-41) *The Handbook of British Birds,* Witherby.

Yeates, G. K. (1948) *Bird Photography,* Faber.

Yorkshire Naturalists' Union (1971) *The Naturalists' Yorkshire,* Dalesman.

Yorkshire Naturalists' Union, *The Naturalist* (Quarterly Journal).

Yorkshire Naturalists' Union, Annual Ornithological Reports.

Some Useful Addresses

FORESTRY COMMISSION: N.E. England Conservancy, 1a Grosvenor Terrace, York.

ROYAL SOCIETY FOR THE PROTECTION OF BIRDS: The Lodge, Sandy, Beds.

R.S.P.B. Reserves in Yorkshire:—

Blacktoft Sands: Andrew Grieve (Warden), Hillcrest, Whitgift, nr. Goole.

Hornsea Mere: Ray Hawley (Warden).

Fairburn Ings: Steve Madge (Warden), 2 Springholme, Caudle Hill, Fairburn, nr. Knottingley.

YORKSHIRE WATER AUTHORITY: Head Office, West Riding House, 67 Albion Street, Leeds.

YORKSHIRE NATURALISTS' TRUST LTD.: 20 Castlegate, York.

Y.N.T. Reserves:—

Spurn: Barry Spence (Warden), Kilnsea, Patrington, nr. Hull.

Wheldrake Ings: Graham Walker (Warden), Sandlands Cottage, Thorganby, York.

YORKSHIRE NATURALISTS' UNION: D. Bramley (Admin. Officer), c/o The Museum, Belle Vue Road, Doncaster.

(The Y.N. Trust Ltd., above, was founded in 1946 as a reserve-owning organisation. The Y.N. Union, established in 1861, is a confederation of scientific and natural history societies. It collects, publishes and keeps records of the county's flora and fauna).

Y.N.U. Annual Ornithological Reports

Editor: J. R. Mather, 44 Aspin Lane, Knaresborough.

Y.N.U. Bird Recorders:

V C 61 D. E. Murray, 36 Warton Avenue, Grove Hill Road, Beverley.

V C 62 R. H. Appleby, 38 Tennyson Avenue, Scarborough.

V C 63 J. E. Dale, 158 Lindley Moor Road, Lindley Moor, Huddersfield.

V C 64 J. R. Mather, 44 Aspin Lane, Knaresborough.

V C 65 B. Shorrock, 7 East View, Settle.

Y.N.U. Spurn Bird Observatory Committee: B. Pashby (Hon. Sec.), 408 Cottingham Road, Hull.

Addresses of the Secretaries of local natural history societies are usually available at the local public library.

The Sparrowhawk